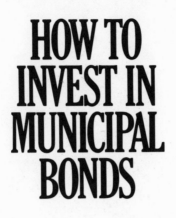

HOW TO INVEST IN MUNICIPAL BONDS

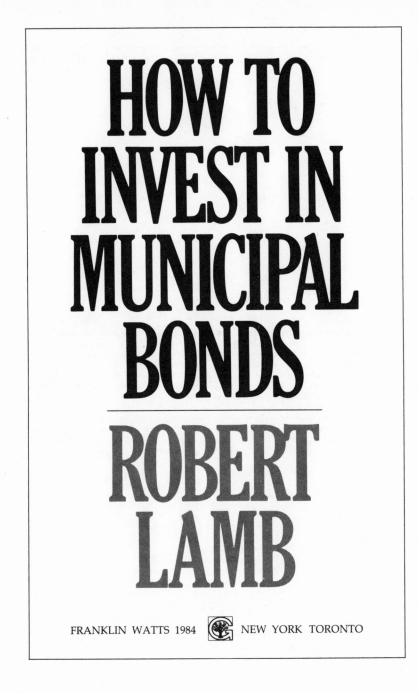

HOW TO INVEST IN MUNICIPAL BONDS

ROBERT LAMB

FRANKLIN WATTS 1984   NEW YORK TORONTO

THIS BOOK IS DEDICATED TO AUSTIN TOBIN

Library of Congress Cataloging in Publication Data

Lamb, Robert.
  How to invest in municipal bonds.

  Includes index.
  1. Municipal bonds—United States—Handbooks,
manuals, etc. I. Title.
HG4952.L35 1984   332.63'233   84-11954
ISBN 0-531-09573-8

ACKNOWLEDGMENTS

This book was written with the advice of many individuals whose day-to-day work involves municipal bond finance. While I take full responsibility for the contents of this volume, I would like to take this opportunity to thank certain individuals whose advice I sought.

High on this list are Heatter Ruth and his colleagues at the Public Securities Association; Edward O'Brien and Robert Royer of the Securities Industry Association; Peter Harkins of the Dealer Bank Association; Donald Beaty and Robert Doty of the Municipal Finance Officers Association; Albert Gordon, Sr., Duncan Gray and Michael Hernandez of Kidder Peabody & Co.; Brenton Harries, John Dailey, Leo O'Neill, Hy Grossman, Richard Huff, Frank Rizzo, Adam Sherman, Steven Joynt, and Vickie Tillman of Standard & Poor's Corporation; the late Jackson Phillips, Freda Ackerman and John Brenner of Moody's; Raymond Lauber of Chase Manhattan Bank; Herman Charbonneau, Charles Adams, and Serefino Tobia of Chemical Bank; John DeJung of the National Securities and Research Corporation; Sylvan Feldstein, Jean Jacques Rousseau, James Cochan and Richard Ackerman of Merrill Lynch Pierce Fenner and Smith, Inc.; Lawrence Caffrey and Joan Camens of Paine Webber Jackson and Curtis; Richard Kolman, Thomas Fegyveresi, Robert Downey, Steven Kinney, Preston Miller, Robert Margolies, and David Darst of Goldman Sachs; Kevin Collins of The First Boston Corporation; Peter Howey and Jerry Fallon of E.F. Hutton; Michael Lipper of Lipper Analytical Distributers; Steven Hueglin of Gabriel Hueglin and Cashman; Russ Frazer and his colleagues at American Municipal Bond Assurance Corporation, and John Butler and his colleagues at Municipal Bond Insurance Association; Richard Cacchione, Thomas Cacchione, William Macarthy, and Arthur Hausker of Fitch Investor Service; Joan Lulkovich and the entire staff of *The Bond Buyer*; Robert Stovall, and Duane Miyagishima of Dean Witter Reynolds; Irvin Goldman of Soloman Brothers; Stephen Tatcher and Daniel Reese of Citicorp; Eileen Austen, and Rhonda Rosenberg of Drexel Burnham Lambert; Richard Moynahan of the Dreyfus Corporation; Frank Wendt, Betty Ganzer, Donald Pitti and Siesel Caraday, Jr., of John Nuveen & Co.; Morgan Murray, William Gibson, and George Friedlander of Smith Barney, Harris Upham; Robert Gerard and Roger Leaf of Morgan Stanley; Michael Hardie of Colonial Management; Thomas Herman of the Wall Street Journal, Scott Hults, David Feinegold, Robert Metz and Paul Steinle of Financial News Network; Andrew Johnson of the Franklin Fund; Peter Gordon of T. Row Price; Michael Bouscaren of Putnam Bond Funds; Kurt Larson of IDS; Robert Broman of Van Kampen Merritt; David Hartman of Federated Bond Funds; Vincent Giordano, Debbie Bernstein, Norman Schevey and Michael Feigeles, all of Merrill Lynch Pierce Fenner and Smith; John Keohane and Donald Robinson of Hawkins Delafield and Wood; Charles Sykes of Willkie Farr & Gallagher; Richard West of Dartmouth's Tuck School; Donna Shalala of Hunter College; Burton Malkiel of the Yale School of Management; James Leighland of the Institute of Public Administration; James Leibenthal, David Lerner and Harrison Golden, Comptroller of New York City; Professors Ingo Walter, Arnold Sametz, Edward Altman, William Silber, Ernest Block, Robert Hawkins, William Guth, Robert Lindsay, Oscar Ornati, Jeremy Wiesen, all of New York University; Steve Ludsin of Erlich Bober; Richard Jenrette of Donaldson, Lufkin and Jenrette; and Edward Alt of The Bank of America.

Enormous amounts of help and advice and research have been provided to me by the entire municipal bond department at Shearson/Lehman/American Express; I am deeply grateful to Robert Adler, Susan Dushock, Harry Waltman, Daniel Berger, Donna DeCoursey-Ordre, Melita Love, Peter Loeb, James Skyrm, James Lynch, Dall Forsyth, Kathy Stewart, Richard Murphy, John Dwyer, Jeffrey Schulsinger, Roland Hauer, Philip Simonetti, Albert Bellas, Richard Bain, Jr. and Joseph Pulmeri and also Robert Topol, of Unit Trust Investments.

Other key individuals who read the entire manuscript to help with its improvement include James Cooner of The Bank of New York; Edie Behr of Dean Witter Reynolds; Stephen Rappaport of Prudential Bache; Austin Tobin of The Delphis Hanover Corporation; and Robert Apfel of Robert Apfel & Co.

My editors Robert Bull, Thomas Rosenbaum, Bernard Axelrod, William Bloor and William Newton deserve my gratitude, as do Melvin Simensky, and my wife, Nancy.

ROBERT LAMB

CONTENTS

vii

PREFACE

Are tax-free municipal bonds an advantageous form of investment for you? You *should* consider these tax-free bonds if you:

- Are in a high tax bracket
- Earn over $18,000 a year
- Are a member of a family with an income of $30,000 or more

What are municipal bonds? They are loans made by citizens to local and state governments as well as to various agencies. The municipalities or agencies use the money for an agreed-upon amount of time, after which they return the principal to the investor. Interest is usually paid semiannually during the life of the loan. Governments and agencies most frequently use the money received from municipal bonds to build roads, schools, and housing, and to finance social programs.

This book will explain a simple step-by-step method by which you can maximize your rate of return and build a tax shelter by purchasing tax-free municipal bonds. The first step is to answer a couple of questions regarding your basic objectives: Are you interested in a short-term or long-term investment? Are you willing to take a greater risk in exchange for the chance to receive a higher yield than you would get from other types of investments?

Because of their tax-free status, municipal bonds offer relatively high yields. On the one hand taxable investments, such as certificates of deposit (CDs) or corporate bonds, may boast a high 15 percent return on your money, but their "real" yield after federal, state, and city taxes may be as low as 8 percent, 7 percent, 6 percent or even less. Tax-free municipal bonds, on the other hand, allow you to keep all the interest.

Municipal bonds do, however, involve certain risks. According to the Joint Economic Committee of the U.S. Congress, "the fiscal health of cities has deteriorated steadily . . . in line with deteriorating economic conditions." Phillip Braverman, vice-president of the Chase Manhattan Bank, warns, "The problems [of municipalities] . . . are so pronounced that they could conceivably push some tax-exempt entities to or beyond the brink of bankruptcy."

If this happened to a bond in which you had invested, you might not recoup your initial investment. Furthermore, a few major municipal defaults might shatter confidence in the whole bond market, causing a loss in market value for all bonds. Before you buy bonds, therefore, you must decide how much risk you can accept. You must then determine which is the safest type of bond and the extent to which liquidity (the ease with which you can sell the bond) is important to you.

There are various ways to reduce the chance of losing money on your tax-free bonds. In today's market, for instance, there is greater opportunity to spread the risk over many rather than a few bond issues. Also, special types of bonds have become available with new features offering inflation protection and backup credit lines.

For example, to guarantee the safety of your asset principal a bank, financial institution, or corporation will sometimes provide a letter of credit. This assures you that you will be paid the full value of your investment even if the government or agency behind the bond cannot pay the interest or principal—for whatever reason. Municipal bond insurance is also available from the Municipal Bond Insurance Association (MBIA) and the American Municipal Bond Assurance Corporation (AMBAC). Of course, the issuance of letters of credit and municipal bond insurance usually results in a high credit rating for the bond, which in turn causes a high demand for it.

In this book, I will show you how to buy municipal bonds wisely and to reduce your risks. I will explain:

- How to understand the risks
- How to minimize and protect yourself from risks
- How to analyze the credit worthiness of municipalities
- How to buy, sell, and swap municipals—whether individually or through mutual funds and trusts or brokers
- How to take strategic losses on your worst securities and to offset taxes against capital gains and income

- How to profit by buying deep-discount bonds
- How to determine which of the new floating-rate bonds are the best, when to avoid them, and why
- How to build wealth via zero coupon bonds

I will show you that, even in this decade of inflation, buying the right municipal bond, as opposed to almost any other security, can still produce a most profitable return. For, despite the risks—taxpayer revolts, sharp cutbacks in certain taxes, and a decrease in federal support for cities—the prospects for most municipal bonds appear bright. Therefore, I will suggest those areas of the bond market that will continue to be the safest and most profitable for the individual investor.

In the first chapters I will break down investment strategy into its crucial stages: how best to buy bonds, how best to sell securities, how best to swap bonds, how best to time your investments, which securities to choose in order to achieve your personal investment goals. Furthermore, I will explain exactly how you can protect yourself against most of the risks of bond investment.

In Chapter 14 you will find comprehensive instructions for mapping out the best possible investment strategy in municipal tax-exempt securities. This chapter summarizes all the advice presented in detail throughout the book.

1

THE VALUE OF TAX-EXEMPT INCOME

It's *not* the amount of your income that counts. It's the amount of income you get to *keep* after you have paid all taxes on that income.

Let's compare the income you earn from two different investments, looking at the *real* income you actually get to keep after you have paid all federal tax, state tax, and local municipal tax on both of those investments. One investment is taxable; the other is not.

For this direct comparison I have chosen your investment of $10,000 in a taxable corporate bond earning 13 percent versus your investment of $10,000 in a tax-free municipal bond earning 10 percent. If you are a New York City resident in the 50 percent tax bracket, then you would immediately see a full 3 percent greater yield, or 30 percent more income before tax, from this taxable bond than from the tax-free municipal security.

However, lets take a closer look at your real income, or real return, from that $10,000 investment in a taxable bond with 13 percent interest.

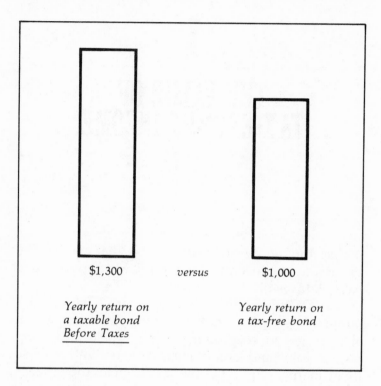

$1,300   *versus* $1,000

Yearly return on   *Yearly return on*
a taxable bond   *a tax-free bond*
Before Taxes

First, Uncle Sam deducts 50 percent of that $1,300 in U.S. federal income tax, which leaves you with $650.

Next, New York State taxes will take an additional $100 of your $1,300 income, leaving you with $550.

Finally, the local government, in this case New York City, will take an additional $50 of your $1,300 income, which leaves you with only $500 in real income after you have paid all taxes on that $1,300. You can actually save, spend, or invest only this $500.

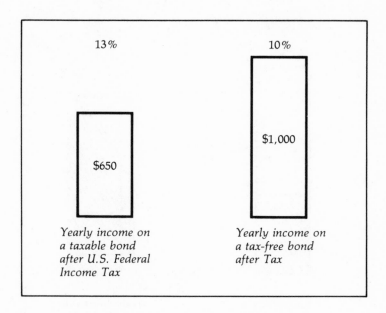

13%   10%

$1,000

$650

Yearly income on
a taxable bond
after U.S. Federal
Income Tax

Yearly income on
a tax-free bond
after Tax

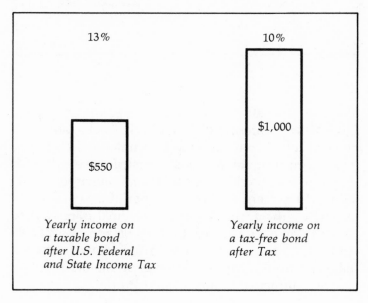

13%   10%

$1,000

$550

Yearly income on
a taxable bond
after U.S. Federal
and State Income Tax

Yearly income on
a tax-free bond
after Tax

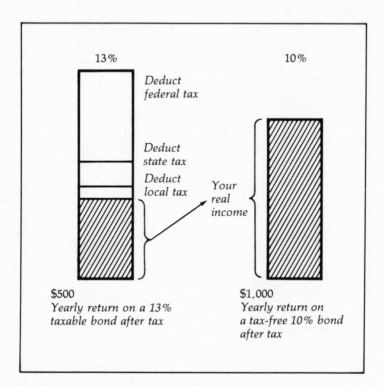

Your real after-tax income per year from your $10,000 investment, then, is $500. That's only a 5 percent return on your money, not the 13 percent return you thought you were going to get.

Compare that low 5 percent real return to the far higher 10 percent real return (after all taxes) offered to you by the triple tax-free municipal bond. *When you invest in tax-free bonds, you keep the money you earn.* And so, as this simple comparison shows, you actually get double the real income when you invest in tax-free municipal bonds.

Try this exercise yourself on *any* investment you own. Use any savings account, CD, U.S. Treasury bill, Treasury bond, Treasury note, corporate bond, or equity stock, and simply write down the exact amount of yearly income you get from it *before* taxes. Then deduct the appropriate federal, state, and city tax for your tax bracket. You'll find tables in Appendices 3, 4, and 5 to help you determine state taxes.

For example, if you are in the 30 percent tax bracket, you will have to find a CD, bond, or stock paying more than 12.5 percent in order to equal what you would earn each year on a 10 percent tax-free municipal bond. If you are in the 35 percent tax bracket, you will have to look for a 15.5 percent CD, bond, or stock in order to equal what you would earn on a 10 percent tax-free bond. In the 40 percent tax bracket, you will need to search for investments earning 16.5 percent to equal what you can earn on a 10 percent tax-free municipal bond. If you are in the 45 percent tax bracket you will be forced to scour the investment market to find a stock, bond, or other investment earning over 18 percent each year in order to equal what you could easily earn on a 10 percent tax-free muni bond. Finally, if you are in the top 50 percent tax bracket, you'll have to search very hard indeed to find an investment that will earn you more than 20 percent a year in order to equal what you could, with no searching at all, earn on any 10 percent tax-free municipal bond.

Obviously, the higher your tax bracket is, the more financial benefit you will gain from investing in tax-free municipal bonds. Millionaires for decades have invested most heavily in tax-free municipals because of the huge advantage they gain by investing in tax-free bonds rather than in CDs, savings accounts, taxable corporate bonds, or taxable government bills, bonds, or notes, or taxable investment returns from dividends on corporate stock.

Conversely, if you are in a very low tax bracket, say 10 to 20 percent, then it makes no sense for you to buy tax-free municipal bonds, for you will earn far higher real returns in taxable securities.

If you are in the 25 to 27 percent tax bracket, then you have a very hard investment decision to make. Is your best choice a taxable investment earning 13 percent or a tax-free investment earning 10 percent? Both will earn you about the same real after-tax return.

In fact, you might think that if you can find a taxable security earning more than 13 percent—say 18 or 20 percent—you will be much better off investing in taxable securities. But such high-yielding taxable investments are usually very risky. So, once again, you are probably better off with a tax-free municipal bond earning 10 percent because it is safer and because you can keep the entire 10 percent interest.

You also must always remember that over the long term your tax bracket may rise—or your state and local taxes may increase—so that the 10 percent tax-free bond that initially was worth only 10 percent to you may in time, as your income rises, be worth 15 or 20 percent or more in terms of a taxable equivalent yield that you could earn on a taxable investment.

Let's see how you can compute your taxable equivalent yield for your investments in your tax bracket. Shearson/American Express developed the following examples for investors in different tax brackets to show what their real taxable equivalent yields from their taxable investments would have to be in order to equal their earnings from a 10 percent tax-free municipal bond.

Since taxes change from year to year, we are providing you with a simple formula that shows what a taxable security would have to yield in order to equal the take-home yield of a tax-exempt municipal bond. Choose any municipal bond yield.

$$\frac{\text{municipal bond yield}}{100\% \text{ minus your } \% \text{ tax bracket}} = \begin{array}{c} \text{taxable} \\ \text{equivalent} \\ \text{yield} \end{array}$$

Here's how it works. Place in the numerator position the interest rate or yield of the municipal bond you are considering. The denominator will be 100 minus your personal tax bracket. Your equation will look something like this:

$$\frac{10\% \text{ municipal bond yield}}{\begin{array}{c}100\% \text{ minus your}\\ \text{tax bracket of } 45\%\end{array}} = \frac{10}{55\%} = 18\% \begin{array}{c}\text{taxable}\\\text{equivalent}\\\text{yield}\end{array}$$

In other words, if you are in the 45 percent tax bracket, you will have to find a taxable investment that will earn you 18 percent or more each year in order to equal what a 10 percent tax-free municipal bond would earn you after all taxes have been paid on that 18 percent investment.

To show you how this might work if you were in different tax brackets, here are some examples (using a 10 percent municipal bond) to show what you would have to earn on a taxable investment to equal what you would earn on a tax-free 10 percent municipal bond.

$$\frac{10\% \text{ municipal bond yield}}{100\% - 25\% \text{ tax bracket}} = 13.3\% \text{ taxable yield}$$

$$\frac{10\% \text{ municipal bond yield}}{100\% - 34\% \text{ tax bracket}} = 15.1\% \text{ taxable yield}$$

$$\frac{10\% \text{ municipal bond yield}}{100\% - 42\% \text{ tax bracket}} = 17.2\% \text{ taxable yield}$$

$$\frac{10\% \text{ municipal bond yield}}{100\% - 50\% \text{ tax bracket}} = 20\% \text{ taxable yield}$$

WHY MUNICIPAL BONDS ARE TAX EXEMPT

Why are tax-free municipal securities of all kinds tax exempt? The reason is quite simple. The law—stemming from the U.S. Constitution and the Supreme Court's interpretations for over a hundred and sixty years—has specified that the federal government cannot tax state and local government securities.

This law is based on a well-known doctrine of constitutional law known as reciprocal immunity, which means that state and local governments cannot tax the federal government, and the federal government in turn cannot tax state or local governments. When you buy U.S. government treasury bills, bonds, or notes you cannot be taxed on that interest income by the states or local government. Likewise, when you buy municipal securities, you cannot be taxed by the federal government on your interest income from those securities.

Ever since a landmark case in 1819, in which Chief Justice John Marshall of the Supreme Court ruled for the plaintiff in *McCulloch* vs. *Maryland*, this doctrine of reciprocal immunity has been upheld. In 1895 in *Polloch* vs. *Farmers Loan and Trust Company* and again in 1916, 1928, 1937, and in 1965, this issue of immunity of state and local securities from federal taxation was upheld in the Supreme Court.

Moreover in 1913, when the first income tax law was passed, Congress made it clear that "Interest upon obligations of a state, territory or any political subdivision thereof is wholly exempt from gross income." The IRS has upheld this ruling ever since.

COULD TAX EXEMPTION END?

Is the tax-exempt status of municipal bonds ever likely to completely change or completely disappear? No. States and municipalities need this tax exemption, for without it they might not get anyone to buy their bonds.

In fact, the investing public might buy few municipal *taxable* securities at all unless these states and communities were willing to offer 14 to 20 percent interest on their bonds. In other words, unless state and local municipalities were able to fully and completely compete with all corporate and government taxable securities in the identical open market, they might not get sold.

In short, without fiendishly high or excessively expensive interest rates offered to entice investors to purchase a small town's bonds or a sewer district's bonds, or even an unstable city's bonds, only a few or perhaps none might be sold.

Although the constitutional case for tax exemption based on the doctrine of reciprocal immunity is solid and is expected to remain secure, the Congress occasionally threatens to disqualify a few types of tax-exempt bonds—certain industrial-revenue bonds, for example, and some other marginal types of tax-free security. For example, the tax-free bonds that are presently under threat of losing their tax-exempt status are industrial-revenue bonds that have been used to finance commercial projects such as McDonald's restaurants or K–Mart shopping centers, which could have been financed by private corporate securities. But the most flagrant abuses involve the use of tax-free industrial-revenue bonds to construct topless bars or pornographic movie theaters or bookstores. Tax-exempt financing was not meant to serve such purposes, and it is these questionable projects that the Congress is considering excluding from tax-exempt financing—not all tax-free municipal bonds.

In June of 1984 the U.S. Senate and the House of Representatives agreed upon a new bill that would set limits or caps on the amount of industrial development revenue bonds (IDBs) that could be issued in each state. The limit on IDBs that could be issued by each state would be a multiple of $150 per person in the state, or $200 million total per state. There were, however, specific exemptions for certain types of bonds from these state limits; for example, for IDBs to finance multi-family housing, mass transit, etc. See Appendix 6.

2

REWARDS OF INVESTING IN TAX-EXEMPT SECURITIES

THREE ADVANTAGES OF TAX-EXEMPT SECURITIES

Many investors think that tax exemption is the only advantage of municipal bonds. The tax exemption *is* crucial, of course, but it is only one of the benefits of municipal bonds, as this chapter will make clear. Municipal bonds have three key advantages:

- Municipal bonds offer potentially larger after-tax returns.
- They require less capital to gain the same dollar amount of return.
- They require a shorter period of time to gain the same return

ALWAYS COMPARE AFTER-TAX RETURNS

Advertisements proclaim "High-Yield 15 Percent CDs" or "Record-High Treasury Bonds, 15.2 Percent." *Re-*

member immediately to subtract half or even more from these alluring claims, because the various governments will take their share according to your tax bracket. The actual yield may be only 9 percent or even lower than 6 percent! Now, compare this return with the advantage you might enjoy from owning some municipals. Even in 1981 and 1982, when interest rates were very high, you could earn nearly twice as much from municipal bonds as you could from taxable securities. Although interest rates were lower in 1983, you could still buy a triple-tax-exempt municipal bond (free from federal, state, and local taxes) with an interest rate of 10 to 13 percent, which could be equivalent to a return of 20 to 30 percent on a taxable return, depending on your bracket.

You can see from Exhibit 1 how you would benefit from investing in tax-exempt bonds or other double- or triple-tax-exempt securities, depending on your income-tax bracket.

Municipal bonds have proved to be one of the safest investments. In fact, municipal bonds are almost as good as direct obligations of the federal government for continuous payment, and they have a much lower incidence of default than corporate bonds. Some tax-free bonds, of course, have defaulted, but most have demonstrated the ability to withstand difficult economic conditions.

COMPARE THE AMOUNT OF CAPITAL YOU MUST INVEST

In many cases, you must invest two to four times the amount of your capital in a taxable investment to earn

EXHIBIT 1

THE VALUE OF FEDERAL TAX EXEMPTION ALONE

Your federal taxable income in thousands		Your federal tax bracket	To match these tax-free rates you would have to earn this much from a taxable investment		
Married	Single		10% Tax Free	13%	
$ 35.2– 45.8	$28.8–34.1	33%–34%	14.92%/15.15%	19.40%/19.69%	
$ 45.8– 60.0	$34.1–41.5	38%	16.12%	20.96%	
$ 60.0– 85.6	$41.5–55.3	42%	17.24%	22.41%	
$ 85.6–109.4	$55.3–81.8	45%–48%	18.18%/19.23%	23.63%/25.00%	
$109.4–162.4		49%	19.60%	25.49%	
$162.4+	$81.8+	50%	20.25%	26.00%	

THE VALUE OF DOUBLE TAX EXEMPTION*

Your taxable income in thousands		Your tax bracket	To match these tax-free rates you would have to earn this much more from a taxable investment	
Married	Single		10% Tax Free	13%
$ 35.2– 45.8	$28.8–34.1	42%/43%	17.24%/17.54%	22.41%/22.80%
$ 45.8– 60.0	$34.1–41.5	47%	18.86%	24.52%
$ 60.0– 85.6	$41.5–55.3	50%	20.00%	26.00%
$ 85.6–109.4	$55.3–81.8	53%/55%	21.27%/22.22%	27.65%/28.88%
$109.4–162.4		56%	22.72%	29.54%
$162.4+	$81.8+	57%	23.25%	30.23%

*Exemption from federal and state income tax.

THE VALUE OF TRIPLE TAX EXEMPTION*

Your taxable income in thousands		Your tax bracket	To match these tax-free rates you would have to earn this much more from a taxable investment	
Married	Single		10% Tax Free	13%
$ 35.2– 45.8	$28.8–34.1	45%/46%	18.18%/18.51%	23.63%/24.07%
$ 45.8– 60.0	$34.1–41.5	49%	19.60%	25.49%
$ 60.0– 85.6	$41.5–55.3	52%	20.83%	27.08%
$ 85.6–109.4	$55.3–81.8	55%/57%	22.22%/23.25%	28.88%/30.23%
$109.4–162.4		58%	23.80%	30.95%
$162.4 +	$81.8 +	59%	24.39%	31.70%

*Exemption from federal, state, and city income taxes.

an amount of income, after taxes, equal to that from
a municipal bond. For example, if you are in the 50
percent federal tax bracket and you live in New York
City (and New York State, which would levy another 9 percent), you would receive interest payments on tax-exempt bonds and other taxable certificates as indicated in the accompanying exhibit.

EXHIBIT 2

	Required cash investment	Before-tax income	After-tax income
10% triple tax-exempt municipal bond	$10,000	$1,000	$1,000
10% U.S. government security	$20,000	$2,000	$1,000
10% CD, or taxable bond	$22,000	$2,200	$1,000
5% dividend on a common stock	$44,000	$2,200	$1,000

This advantage of municipals becomes even
greater as interest rates rise. Therefore, you should
carefully weigh the size of your commitment against
that of any alternative investment. Your capital is hard
earned, and valuable so make each dollar work to the
maximum. Keep your income tax bracket in mind
before you invest in any taxable investment!

COMPARE LENGTH OF TIME
YOU MUST TIE UP YOUR CAPITAL

In this age of high interest rates and uncertainty, the
length of time that you tie up your money may affect

your ability to sell holdings without suffering a penalty. Instead of locking yourself into a thirty-year bond, you may wish to take advantage of more lucrative alternatives next year, which might not be offered at a later date. Also, when you lock yourself into a long-term bond, you run the risk of being paid years later in dollars that might have depreciated over time. Therefore, you should remember that you do not need to tie up your money for a long period of time.

If you want only short-term securities, you can buy a whole range of tax-free money market funds, tax-free notes, tax-free municipal commercial paper. These can be short-term tax-free securities with maturity dates that are only a few days, weeks, or months in the future or that are one to three years away, at most.

You might want to consider longer-term tax-free notes or tax-free bonds in the one- to six-year range. Or you could achieve this same shorter-term financial flexibility by investing, for example, in put bonds, which are explained later. If you buy a put bond, you can sell the security back to the issuer at par before maturity. Usually, the put can be exercised on a yearly basis beginning three to five years after it is issued. It is up to you to decide whether to sell the bond or retain it to maturity. With some bonds, you can safeguard your liquidity and ensure very high returns as well.

Investment in various tax-free notes can earn you as much money in a year as the same investment in taxed securities would produce in two or three years (after taxes). The following table compares the length of time you would have to tie up $10,000 to earn $1,000 after-tax income.

Investment of $10,000	Time needed to earn $1,000
10% tax-exempt municipal bond	1 year
10% CD, or taxable bond	2 years, 5 months
5% dividend on common stock	4 years, 1 month

In times of steep inflation and rapidly deflating dollars, you should avoid locking yourself into long-term bonds. As a means of avoiding losses, look instead at put bonds, short-term tax-exempt notes, tax-free money market funds, and municipal commercial paper lasting only a few months or weeks.

You might consider another form of investment to avoid the penalties of fluctuating interest rates—floating-rate or variable-rate bonds. These bonds provide an interest rate that is adjusted to the prevailing interest rates. Usually this variable-rate bond is adjusted quarterly and based on the rates yielded by ninety-one-day U.S. Treasury bills and thirty-year U.S. Treasury bonds, and estimated by private analysts.

INVESTING IN DOUBLE- OR TRIPLE-TAX-EXEMPT BONDS

You can buy tax-exempt bonds issued by the city or state in which you live and enjoy exemptions from local, state, and federal taxes. This is the triple tax exemption. If you are a resident of Texas, Nevada,

Alaska, South Dakota, or Wyoming, you will not have to pay state tax on income from bonds issued by other states. Some other states and localities levy negligible taxes on bonds, no matter where they originate.

However, buying bonds in your own state to get triple tax exemption may *not* be the best way to enhance your profits in all cases. Many out-of-state bond issues might give you a higher return after your state taxes than those issued by your state. Therefore, even though California residents have to pay taxes on interest they receive from bonds issued by other states, the tax differential may be small because they can deduct their state tax from their federal income tax.

Your *effective tax rate* is the actual amount of state tax you pay on municipal bond income after deducting your state tax from your federal tax. To illustrate, let's say that a California resident in the 50 percent marginal federal tax bracket earns $100 in interest income on a bond she holds from another state—say, New York—and this bond has a face value of $1,000. She would pay California taxes of 11 percent of her interest income, or $11 on the $100. However, she can deduct her California tax from her federal taxable income, and that will reduce her federal tax by $5.50 on that $11—or, in other words, by 50 percent. Her effective yield on this 10 percent bond is 9.45 percent ($100 − $5.50 ÷ $1,000) or a difference of only .55 percent or 55 basis points.

Thus, if the yield differential is wide enough, it might be worthwhile to buy bonds from out of state even though you lose the triple tax exemption. The state and local tax on your out-of-state municipal bonds exceeds .5 percent in only twenty-one states.

Since you can often make 1 or even 2 percent more on your total investment on these out-of-state municipal bonds than you can on bonds from your own state, it is possible that you could earn a good deal more tax-free income if you buy out-of-state bonds.

You should also note, however, that some states *do* levy heavy taxes. The total combined taxes of some states and municipalities range from 10 to 19 percent, and even if you deduct this from your federal tax, your effective extra tax on top of your federal tax could be a hefty 5 to 9 percent. Other states—Ohio, for example—impose an additional "gains tax" or "personal property tax" on top of your federal and state income taxes. It is clear that investing in out-of-state bonds makes little sense if you live in these states. Check Appendices 3, 4, and 5, at the end of this book, for each state's tax.

WHAT IF THE FEDERAL GOVERNMENT IMPOSES AN INCOME-TAX SURCHARGE OR OTHER NEW TAXES ON INCOMES OVER $50,000 OR OVER $100,000?

If you are a millionaire, or if you hope to become one, you may worry about Congress imposing an income-tax surcharge. What if Congress raises the top tax bracket to above 50 percent because of a new tax? How much greater might your incentive be to invest in municipal bonds in the future? Alternatively, how likely is it that today's tax bracket ceiling of 50 percent will stay in effect long into the future?

If state and local taxes remain at current levels, and if the 50 percent ceiling continues at the federal level, the highest total of combined state and local taxes would amount to 22 percent. Even after the deduction of this amount from your federal income tax, you still would have to pay 8 to 12 percent in effective actual tax on top of your 50 percent federal tax. Therefore, you might still find yourself paying 60 percent in combined federal, state, and local taxes on your taxable securities. This is indeed better than the previous top combined rate of 75 percent, but it is not very much less. Thus it is clearly still worth your while to look into municipal securities for that tax-free or after-tax yield.

3

MUNICIPAL BOND MARKETS AND THE TYPES OF MUNICIPAL BONDS

MUNICIPAL BOND MARKETS

Municipal bonds are offered to investors through *primary* and *secondary markets.* The primary market offers new bond issues. The secondary market trades in bonds that have already been issued and are now being submitted for resale. The *retail market* is that portion of the overall market oriented to individual investors to buy, sell, or swap bonds in order to improve their portfolios. Most municipal bond transactions are effected *over the counter*—in other words they are accomplished by a phone call to a dealer or through bank trust departments or investment advisory firms.

There, also, is a *wholesale market* where dealers and institutions trade large blocks of bonds. Although major financial institutional buyers account for only about 25 percent of the new bond issues being sold, they are constantly adjusting their holdings of older bond issues to take advantage of new investment opportunities in higher-yield bonds. Even though institutional buyers may take only a small part of the new bonds issued, they serve to set prices of bonds in both the primary and secondary markets because, when they do buy or sell, they do so in large blocks and their transactions are highly visible. For example, one firm alone, the All-State Insurance Company, increased its bond holdings by $600 million in 1977. That was equivalent to about 1 percent of all bonds then offered publicly.

The New-Issue Municipal Bond Market

By 1984 over 100,000 municipalities, cities, states, school districts, and public authorities had issued securities worth over $400 billion.

Of the new issues, about 30 percent were *general-obligation bonds* (GO bonds) issued by states, cities, and municipalities and backed by their full faith and credit and the taxing power. However, most of the tremendous new growth in the municipal bond market is not due to GOs issued by municipalities. Fully 70 percent of all new bonds sold are *not* backed by *ad valorem* taxes, but instead are revenue bonds usually backed by revenues derived from the operation of some municipal project, such as a toll road, or user taxes. This is a dramatic change from twenty years ago when over 70 percent of all municipal bonds issued were GO bonds backed by taxes. This has been brought about by the proliferation of revenue-bond-issuing authorities and agencies. These public-revenue authorities are usually empowered by legislation to contract debts payable from fees, tolls, or service charges. They issue *revenue bonds*, the proceeds from which are used to build and operate parking lots, tunnels, airports, seaports, rapid transit systems, and other public projects.

Recently there has been a dramatic rise in the sale of *industrial-revenue bonds,* which are ultimately backed by corporations rather than by a government or agency. They are used for projects such as new plants and warehouses. They also have been issued for commercial projects including stores, malls, and office buildings. Such projects can be financed by municipal bonds if they provide new employment opportunties in depressed areas or otherwise aid some public purpose. (See Appendix 6 for limits.)

New issues of municipal bonds (whether general-obligation bonds or revenue bonds) are usually brought to the public debt markets because the municipality or public authority cannot finance all its buildings or enter into all its new projects with its currently available tax receipts or user-fee revenues and because it often makes sense to finance long-term assets (buildings) with long-term liabilities (bonds).

Municipalities persuade investment bankers, commercial banks, or other financial firms to act as underwriters of the new municipal issue. Usually such banks or investment banks will work together in syndicates. They will make a bid to the municipality in an attempt to win the bonds competitively or to negotiate the contract to underwrite this new issue of bonds. Most general-obligation bond issues today are sold by competitive bidding between such syndicates of investment banking firms. Most revenue bonds are *not* sold by competitive bidding between syndicates but, instead, are directly negotiated with only one syndicate or one financial firm.

Each bid by a syndicate (in competitive or negotiated bidding) is in effect an offer to buy the entire new issue of bonds at one set price from the municipality.

The firms in the syndicate that are chosen to underwrite the bonds then have the right to sell the new bonds to wholesale or retail customers. The underwriters' "spread," or profit, is the difference between the price that the syndicate agrees to pay for the bonds and the price at which the syndicate offers to sell the bonds to the public.

TYPES OF MUNICIPAL BONDS

You can invest in a number of different types of tax-exempt municipal securities:

1. General-obligation municipal bonds backed by the issuer's guarantee to pay the principle and interest from tax income on real property without limitation as to rate or amount.
2. General-obligation municipal notes issued for short terms and also backed by such taxes.
3. General-obligation municipal leases for buildings or equipment backed by the taxing power.
4. Limited and special tax bonds backed by a guarantee to pay the principal and interest from a special tax on, say, gasoline, cigarettes, liquor, betting, or assessments.
5. Revenue bonds backed by a promise from a city, state, special authority, or agency established to construct and/or operate tunnels, hospitals, or other public facilities, to pay the

principal and interest from tolls, revenues, or rental income.

6. Letter-of-credit–backed bonds backed by an irrevocable guarantee from a bank or institution other than the issuer.

7. Double-barreled bonds backed by a pledge from two or more sources, such as the proceeds of a special tax *and* the general obligation pledge of the state that issues the bonds.

8. Housing bonds backed by mortgage payments or rents on the property developed, or sometimes backed by government-guaranteed loans and insurance.

9. Bonds insured by
    - The Municipal Bond Insurance Association (MBIA) or the American Bond Assurance Corporation (AMBAC), both of which are backed by different groups of insurance companies. MBIA and AMBAC fully insure the payment of principal and interest to institutional and private investors. The bonds they cover are, accordingly, given an AAA rating by Standard & Poor's.
    - The Financial Guarantee Insurance Corporation (FGIC).
    - Other specialized insured bonds such as Health Industry Bond Insurance (HIBI) for hospitals.

10. Project notes issued by a local authority for a particular project, such as low-income housing, backed by the authority and secured by the federal government.

11. Short-term municipal notes issued for one year

or for one to three years. The most common tax-free notes are those backed by anticipated taxes, revenues, or the proceeds of future bond sales.

12. Tax-free municipal commercial paper sold for a very short term: fifteen days to forty-five days, for example.

13. Tax-exempt bond funds and unit trusts. Tax-exempt bond funds are established by brokerage companies in order to buy bonds and issue shares to investors in the fund on securities bought, sold, or traded. Unit trusts are similar, except that their managers cannot trade their bonds before maturity.

BOND CREDIT RATINGS

Many tax-exempt municipal bonds and notes are given ratings to indicate their degree of credit worthiness security from risk or default. Three major national rating agencies analyze the securities and the creditworthiness of the municipal authorities issuing bonds. They are Moody's Investor Service, Standard & Poor's Corporation, and Fitch Investors Service. (Moody's and Standard & Poor's also will rate short-term issues.) Small issues of municipal bonds and notes are often sold without a credit rating.

These rating agencies rely on internal analysis and consult with the municipality, with the issuer's accountants, and with lawyers. They also consult the various bond underwriters. The ratings are reviewed periodically, based on the credit worthiness of the issuing authority at the time as well as on economic conditions. The nomenclature for ratings varies among the different agencies. However, each assesses a bond on a scale from "high" to "low," or most secure to least secure—or prime to default. The following table shows the agencies' ratings.

Credit worthiness	Moody's	Standard & Poor's and Fitch
Prime (highest quality debt)	Aaa	AAA
Excellent	Aa	AA
Good	A	A
Average	Baa	BBB
Fair	Ba	BB
Poor	B	—
Marginal	Caa	B
Default	C	D

Bonds rated between prime and average are considered "investment grade" by banks and conservative investors. Those rated below average are considered "speculative" by the same investors.

In addition, Standard & Poor's has added plus and minus signs to the ratings of certain securities in order to differentiate between stronger and weaker credit ratings. This was done because there were so many bonds in each category. Similarly, Moody's adds a number one to the ratings of bonds that possess the strongest attributes in a category. For example, the strongest bonds in the Aa category are rated Aa1, the strongest bonds in the A category are rated A1, and the strongest bonds in the Baa category are rated

Baa1. Moody's ratings for short-term notes appear in the following list:

- MIG 1—Loans bearing this designation are of the best quality, enjoying strong protection from established cash flows of funds for their servicing or from established and broad-based access to the market for refinancing, or both.
- MIG 2—Loans bearing this designation are of high quality, with margins of protection ample although not so large as in the preceding group.
- MIG 3—Loans bearing this designation are of favorable quality, with all security elements accounted for but lacking the undeniable strength of the preceding grades. Market access for refinancing, in particular, is likely to be less well established.
- MIG 4—Loans bearing this designation are of adequate investment quality carrying specific risk but having protection commonly regarded as required of an investment security and not distinctly or predominantly speculative.

KEY CHARACTERISTICS OF MUNICIPAL BONDS

Municipal bonds, like many debts investments, have a number of characteristics in common: cash is invested; a coupon or interest rate is earned periodically; a maturity date is established on which the bond becomes due; call features may exist to enable issuers to pay off the bond at an early date.

To be really successful as a sophisticated investor in municipal bonds you must understand the more specific characteristics of municipal bonds. They include credit ratings, levels of quality, yield to maturity and current yield, after capital gains tax yield, security or pledged backing behind the bonds, details of sinking fund and call provisions, marketability, liquidity, and the actual type of bonds, such as revenue bonds for hospitals, housing, public power, and general-obligation bonds for states, cities, and school districts, among many others.

The major characteristics of municipal bonds can be summarized to provide you with the information you need to know for successful investing and to maximize your tax-exempt income.

Principal
The principal is the face value of a bond; it is not the amount of capital or cash that you invest in that bond. The principal amount is returned to you at the final maturity date (or redemption date) stated on the face of the bond, no matter what your purchase price was. The principal amount of the municipals is referred to in terms of $1,000. However, most bonds are sold in denominations of $5,000. Bonds of smaller denominations are sometimes sold by a municipality that seeks a broader market for its securities. These are known as baby bonds, mini bonds, or citizen bonds. In most cases a bond is described in terms of $1,000, so a bond with a face value of $100,000 is referred to as one hundred bonds. Institutions and wealthy individuals trade in "round lots" of twenty-five bonds or one hundred bonds each. Smaller numbers of bonds are called "odd lots."

Municipal bonds may be in bearer form, registered form, or book entry citizen-bond form. New federal legislation requires that all new issues of municipal bonds after July 1, 1983, be in registered form. Generally speaking, until 1983 the vast majority of municipal bonds were bearer bonds, which meant that the principal and interest were payable to the person who had possession of the bonds and who presented the bond or coupon when due or called. Registered bonds provide greater safety to the investor, because payments are made only to the person whose name is registered in the file of the issuer. They are convenient because interest checks are sent directly to the holder of record. Bearer or unregistered coupon bonds, however, were easier to market.

Because of this new federal law that requires all municipal bonds issued after July 1983 to be in registered form, there may eventually be a dramatic increase in the efficiency with which these new registered bonds are stored, shipped, counted, and sold. The older bearer bonds had to be counted and handled by hand; the new ones will be done by computer. This new efficiency may lead to cost savings and a broader bond market for all investors. For the moment, however, bearer bonds still possess a better secondary market or "resale value."

Maturities

There are two basic types of maturities: serial maturities, term bonds.

Serial maturities are those portions of a bond issue that come due year after year in specific amounts over an extended period of time. This key feature is especially important in attracting retail investors and certain banks into the municipal bond market, as will be discussed in the following chapter.

Term bonds, or dollar bonds, are those that mature on a single date well into the future. These bonds are often issued on behalf of revenue-producing governments and authorities such as those organized to finance toll roads, utilities, housing authorities, bridge and tunnel authorities, hospitals, or pollution-abatement facilities. Dollar bonds have only one coupon and one fixed maturity date. As the name suggests, they are quoted on a dollar price (or percentage of par) rather than on a yield-to-maturity basis. The most common method of revenue bond financing involves offering a greater amount of long-term (or dollar-bond) debt than of serial debt. As a result, many Wall Street firms maintain more active markets in dollar bonds. Therefore, dollar bonds are generally more marketable than serial bonds are, and the odd-lot differential applied against the individual seller is somewhat less. These bonds usually are retired with money from a sinking fund, which is basically a means by which the issuer makes periodic payments to the paying agent or trustee who, in turn, redeems a portion of the bonds either through purchases in the open market or by lottery. The issuer who redeems by lot pays at least par or face value.

Call Provisions

Outstanding bonds may be retired through call provisions, or the purchase of bonds before their maturity date. Bonds may be callable at a price established when the bonds first were issued, par or at a premium over par. For instance, a $100 par value bond, which is callable at $103, means that the issuer pays $1,030 to you, the bondholder, when you relinquish your $1,000 bond. The premium paid usually decreases in stages, depending on how long the bond has been outstanding, to par, over a period of years. Although some call provisions are mandatory, the bonds may have optional calls for the issuing body to "prepay" the bonds in full or in part. Municipal bonds often have "call protection" for the investor, which means the bonds cannot be retired before a certain number of years, usually five to ten. Investors receive a premium over par for callable bonds as call protection, and this offers a shield for investors as interest rates drop.

BUYING MUNICIPAL BONDS

Discount Bonds

Discount bonds include any bonds that are selling below the $1,000 par value originally printed on the bonds. Years later when they reach their final maturity date these discount bonds will be paid back in full at $1,000. Therefore discount bonds rise in value at final maturity date to par of $1,000. This rise in value would be considered a long-term capital gain, for income tax purposes. In other words, if you buy a $10,000 bond at $8,500 and sell it three years later for $9,500, your $1,000 profit is taxable as a capital gain. These bonds must also be amortized for tax purposes. This means that if your bond increases in value by $1,000 in three years, you must recognize $333.33 of earnings in each separate year. See your accountant for specific taxes you may owe on bonds bought at a discount. Also remember that you may owe federal, state, and local tax on some discount bonds.

Original-Issue Discount

Some bonds are sold at a discount when originally issued. The return is thus based on both coupon and capital appreciation. The amount that is received at a later time when the bonds mature is not taxable as a capital gain and is regarded as tax-exempt income for the investor if held to maturity and officially qualified as original issue discounts. Original-issue discounts can also be purchased in the secondary markets. The buyer picks up that part of the accretion that is unexpired.

Premium Bonds

Generally speaking, bonds bought by investors in the secondary market at a premium, namely those that are bought at a price above par value, will not be considered a capital loss if they are held to maturity and redeemed at par value. Note, however, that as a taxpayer you are required to amortize the premium you paid for the tax-exempt bonds over the life of the issue. For instance, if you bought a $1,000 bond that was set to mature in twenty years at $1,200, you would, on your tax return, have to reduce the cost basis of the bond by $10 each year for the twenty years. If you sell your bond after five years for $1,150, you *cannot* take that $50 as a loss on your tax return from your original $1,200 premium price. See your accountant for the tax implications of sales of specific tax-free bonds bought at a premium.

Coupon

The coupon is the stated value of the rate of return on the bond. For example, an 8 percent coupon rate printed on your bond *simply* means that 8 percent is the rate of interest to be paid on the full $1,000 principal stated amount on your bond. This coupon is usually fixed at a set level to be paid semiannually or annually, but it can be set to a floating rate. If that is done, the rate of return can move either up or down by small intervals once or twice a year, usually pegged to the interest rate on U.S. securities, which tend to move up and down with changes in Federal Reserve Board monetary policy, changes in the GNP, and changes in inflation rates. Bonds that return interest based on floating rates tend not to have coupons as high as fixed-coupon bonds, and most professional portfolio managers avoid them, since their price rarely is sufficient to match a fixed-coupon bond.

It is important to understand that low-coupon (or discount) bonds have far wider swings in price than higher-coupon (current coupon or premium) bonds. These wide swings in price (known as high volatility) make low-coupon bonds behave quite differently from higher-coupon bonds.

In the case of deep discounts, it takes a smaller movement to achieve a change (rise or fall) in the dollar price. For example, a 50 basis point decline in the market rates will produce a much more significant increase in the dollar price of a deep discount bond than it would in the price of a current coupon bond.

These two distinct characteristics provide strategic advantages for investors willing to swap into and out of different types of bonds in order to capture the highest yield on the upturn or downturn in interest rate cycles.

Current Yield

Current yield is the actual yield an investor is receiving. This takes into account the cost of the bond as it relates to the coupon rate. The general formula is as follows:

$$\text{Current yield} = \frac{\text{coupon yield (annual interest payment)}}{\text{current market price of bond}}$$

For instance, the current yield of a bond with a maturity value of $5,000 with a coupon rate of 8 percent that was purchased at a discount of $4,800 would be

$$\frac{\$5,000 \times 8\%}{\$4,800} = \frac{\$400}{\$4,800} = \frac{1}{12} = 8.33\%$$

Similarly a bond worth $5,000 at maturity selling at $5,600 and thus carrying a premium with a coupon of 8 percent would have a current yield of:

$$\frac{\$5,000 \times 8\%}{\$5,600} = \frac{\$400}{\$5,600} = \frac{1}{14} = 7.14\%$$

Yield to Maturity

Municipal bonds are bought and sold on the basis of yield to maturity or yield to call. The most common evaluation of a bond issue is based on the yield to maturity. This figure provides you, the investor, with the return on the bond if held to maturity. If you purchase a bond at par, the yield to maturity would be the same as the coupon yield. In the secondary market, bonds may be purchased at par, but more often at a discount or premium, so the yield to maturity is usually different from the coupon rate.

The yield to maturity is not a fixed or flat rate. Because you receive interest payments semiannually or annually, it has been somewhat unreasonably assumed that you are always able to reinvest your interest payments at the same rate of interest (as the coupon or the bond).

Your yield to maturity on this bond varies with the rate of reinvestment return you make on each of the interest payments you receive every six months. Therefore, the actually realized yield to maturity can be higher or lower than common usage indicates.

The formula used to compute yield to maturity is as follows:

1. Average annual return on investment =
annual interest ±
prorated discount or prorated premium

2. Average investment cost $= \dfrac{\text{purchase price} + \text{maturity cost}}{2}$

3. Yield to maturity = ½ of
$$\dfrac{\text{average annual return on investment}}{\text{average investment cost}}$$

Here is an example. If you buy a $1,000 bond maturing in twenty years at $980, and this bond carries a coupon of 8 percent, what is its yield to maturity?

1. $80 [annual interest] + $4 [prorated discount (80 ÷ 20)] = $84 annual interest return

2. $\dfrac{\$980 + \$1,000}{2} = \dfrac{\$1,980}{2} = \dfrac{\$990 \text{ average}}{\text{investment cost}}$

3. $\dfrac{84}{990} = 8.484\%$

Now suppose that you buy a $1,000 bond that will mature in thirty years. You purchase the bond today at $1,020, and it carries a coupon of 9 percent. What is its yield to maturity?

1. $\$90 - (20/30) = \$89.33$ annual interest

2. $\dfrac{1,020 + 1,000}{2} = \dfrac{2,020}{2} = \$1,010 \ \begin{array}{l}\text{average}\\\text{investment}\\\text{cost}\end{array}$

3. $\dfrac{89.33}{1,010} = 8.845\%$

Accrued Interest

Municipal bonds are bought and sold with accrued interest so that the purchaser of the bond pays the seller the interest earned on the bond from the time of the last coupon date up to, but *not* including the settlement date. Interest is paid semiannually for most municipal bonds and is computed on a 360-day basis so that the buyer never pays more than 179 days' interest. Also remember that each month is considered to have only 30 days for the purposes of calculating accrued interest on municipal bonds.

The following formula is used to compute accrued interest:

$$\text{Accrued Interest} = \text{principal amount} \times$$
$$\text{coupon rate} \times \frac{\text{days}}{360}$$

A $100,000 bond purchase with an 8 percent coupon rate and ninety days' interest would have an accrued interest equivalent to

$$\$100,000 \times 8\% \times \frac{90}{360} = \$2,000$$

Yield Measurements

There is no single definition of yield. Therefore, any given calculation of yield, or rate of return, is related to a specific situation and the specific techniques employed in measuring it. "Yield to maturity," "yield to call," "net interest cost," "Canadian interest cost," "true interest cost," "running yield," "current yield," and other terms denote some of the different measurements of overall return that are used by buyers, dealers, brokers, underwriters, or issuers.

Each different class of participants in the municipal bond market may use a different set of yield calculations and measurements of return because of their quite different needs or requirements. Certain market participants, however, are required by law to use a specific measure of yield. For example, underwriters of bonds are usually instructed by state laws or the notice of sale to use net interest cost (NIC) or true interest cost (TIC). Net interest cost is a way to measure a municipality's expense for paying yield to investors. Because "net interest" is a technical term largely of concern to professional bond underwriters and bond issuers, I will not cover it here. For a more detailed definition, see my book *Municipal Bonds* (New York: McGraw-Hill, 1980).

Bond traders and investors, however, tend to think in terms of "yield to maturity" or "yield to call." The calculation of yield to maturity was long thought to be simple and accurate; however, it is perhaps not so, because the actual yield to maturity always depends on the interest rate at which you, the investor, can reinvest the coupons when you receive them. If you cannot get a rate of interest for the coupons as high as the original yield rate on the bonds, then your actual yield to maturity will be lower than the stated yield to maturity. If you can get a higher interest rate at which to reinvest the coupons, then the actual yield to maturity will be far higher. The range of yields to maturity on exactly the same bond is quite considerable.

"Current yield" or "running yield" is another popular measure of return and is simply the coupon rate divided by the price of the bond. It is a useful measure of a bond's current value if the private investor or the professional wants current income. However, yield to maturity or yield to call provides a better guide for everyone.

Yield to call is yet another measure of a bond's return. Many municipal bonds are callable, and some may have more than one possible call date. A "call" is a payment of the principal of the bond back to the bondholder at a time well in advance of the maturity date printed on the bond. As already noted, if the bond issuer calls the bond, the investor has the problem of reinvesting the principal at a rate of return equivalent to or better than the rate of return received under the old bond. The current rate of interest may be lower than the rate the investor was getting on the bond, which is one primary reason why bonds are called and why refunding of bonds has become so popular with issuers.

PRICE AND YIELD

Municipal bonds display a higher degree of price fluctuation than other fixed-income securities during times when interest rates are increasing or decreasing. Part of the reason for this is that when interest rates move down and money becomes available, commercial banks and other such institutions buy large amounts of new municipal issues. Conversely, when interest rates climb and money is scarcer, banks and financial institutions sell their municipal bonds in an effort to make money available for loans. The reaction of each bank will vary, however, depending on the state of its portfolio, its need for tax-exempt income, its liquidity, and other factors.

You must be aware of two vitally important principles: (1) when interest rates fall, the price of *previously sold* municipal bonds rises, and when interest rates rise, the price of *previously sold* municipal bonds falls; and (2) when a municipal bond is purchased at a discount, or for less than its par value, its current yield is less than its yield to maturity and greater than the coupon rate.

PRICE VOLATILITY AND MATURITY

Chart-watching of bond behavior demonstrates clearly, over time, that bonds which will not mature for many years are far more volatile than short-term bonds. This volatility exists quite simply because there is a far greater likelihood, over the life of the long-term bond, that changes in interest rates will affect the bond's value. Thus if you watch two separate bonds of the same issue but of drastically different maturities, you will see that the long-term bond will be more volatile or change more in price level than will the short-term security.

As previously explained, bonds purchased at a discount in the secondary market tend to be more volatile in price than par bonds or premium bonds. Bonds selling at a premium tend to be more stable in price than par bonds. Therefore we can see from chart observations of different types of bonds over time that greater volatility is associated with low-coupon bonds, long-maturity bonds, and discount bonds. As prices fluctuate in response to interest-rate changes, substantial chances will arise for investors both to make and to lose money.

Conversely, greater stability of bond price is associated with high-coupon bonds trading near par, short-maturity bonds or notes, and bonds selling at a premium over par. If you keep these behavior patterns of bonds in mind, you might be able to profit by swapping one type of bond for another when interest-rate cycles drive the more volatile bonds either upward or downward.

CREDIT AND SECURITY FEATURES

Municipal bonds such as project notes backed by the federal government tend to sell at the very lowest yield because they are very safe and have a low ratio of risk to reward. In addition, project notes are highly marketable and can be converted to cash with little risk of loss. Likewise AAA general-obligation bonds tend to sell at lower yields than AA bonds, and AA bonds sell at lower yields than A bonds. However, although there is a general rule of thumb that the lower the credit quality of the bond the higher the yield and vice versa, *the exceptions are legion.* Overvalued AA bonds and undervalued A bonds, for example, can be identified, as can undervalued A-rated bonds that are quite likely to become AA-rated and vice versa. Remember that in most cases the higher the credit quality of the bond, the lower the yield you can expect to earn.

It is also important for all municipal bond investors to realize that within each investment grade there are great variations in underlying credit value, and variations in price. These relationships between bond price and bond credit quality are by no means always in line with each other, and therefore it is possible to find the one undervalued security within a credit rating category that actually has far stronger credit backing or underlying backup security than other bonds in that same credit rating category. Another reason that the search for undervalued bonds can be so important is that ratings on each municipal bond issuer will be revised periodically. If a bond's rating is raised, the price and ultimate value of those bonds will immediately rise. Forecasting or outguessing the rating agencies on such anticipated rating changes is a favorite game of many municipal bond analysts.

Credit quality can be split between the underlying strength of the municipality and its ability to pay its debts, and special features of the bond agreement (if there are any) that may provide additional layers of security for the bondholder. The underlying strength of the AA-rated credit of Triborough Bridge and Tunnel Authority, for example, would lie in its ability to generate toll revenues. Other special features of bonds that have been structured specifically to give more credit protection to bondholders include mandatory call features, sinking funds, various types of guarantees by federal or state authorities, special contingency agreements, and special contractual arrangements.

The most typical are call features and sinking funds. They can strengthen a bond by cutting down the outstanding debt and reducing the "average life" of the bond. At a certain time, the issuer can repurchase the bonds with a fund kept specifically for that purpose.

A sinking fund guarantees that the weighted average life of all the bonds in the issue is shortened. You may wonder how likely it is your bond might be called or bought back by the manager of the sinking fund. In short, you should consider the effect of shortened average maturity. To measure this, you may wish either to calculate the yield on the bonds against the average life of the bond or to calculate the yield to the first call date. Although a sinking fund call provision does provide credit support for the bonds, it also may jeopardize your long-term expected yield, because if your bonds are called, you have no guarantee that you can reinvest the proceeds of your redeemed bonds at anything like the yield available at the time on the bonds that have just been called. Also this credit quality feature of a call can reduce the ultimate yield that you can expect to earn on a bond. This is another example of the risk-return tradeoff. The less risk you take—or the more credit security you have—the lower your return will be.

4

BUILDING A PORTFOLIO OF MUNICIPAL BONDS

All too many investors forget two basic questions: Why did I invest in the first place? and, What are my primary goals? Many people have not even thought about these questions. Yet, it is not enough merely to aim for high yield or high income as a single goal. You must take many considerations into account as you try to determine the goal you want to reach through investing. And there are many ways you can achieve these goals. There is no all-purpose, all-inclusive investment strategy that is right for all investors.

You must assess both the goals you want to reach and how you might fulfill them. Many investors ask the following questions:

INVESTOR'S QUIZ

- What is my goal for investing? Maximum income? Capital appreciation? Safety of asset principle? Tax shelter?

- How much time am I willing to spend learning about my investment alternatives and managing my portfolio?
- What exactly is my municipal bond income to be used for? Spending? My retirement in five years? Children's college education? Reinvestment?
- How much income do I need for living expenses from this bond investment?
- How soon do I need to retrieve the invested principal?
- What minimum rate of return after taxes will I accept from my investment?
- What are my fears about investing in municipal bonds rather than in the stock market or in real estate?
- How much risk am I willing to take?
- Are there areas in the United States that I do not wish to invest in.
- Do I object to investing in certain types of bonds such as nuclear power plant bonds, remote hospitals, or low-income housing?
- How liquid or quickly convertible into cash must my investments be?
- How long do I want the maturity on my bonds to stretch?
- How marketable must my securities be or how large a number of buyers must be available in order for me to feel comfortable if I have to sell my bonds?
- Do I want well-known bonds only or would I buy little-known special bonds?
- Do I prefer only short-term notes?
- What *after-tax* rate of return would I earn if I

had invested in bank CDs, money market funds, savings accounts, Treasury bills, bonds, or notes, corporate bonds, or the stock market?

- What is my tax bracket today? What do I expect it to be in two years? Five years? Ten years?
- Would I prefer to invest in municipal bonds, tax-free notes, tax-free leases, tax-free bond funds, or unit trusts?

It is vital for you to determine the answers to these questions. Set your goals and choose the best means to achieve them. Some examples of what you might decide to do follow.

INVESTING FOR HIGH YIELD

If you wish to receive a maximum tax-exempt income from municipal bonds, then you should buy hospital bonds, industrial development bonds, and special project revenue bonds.

Here are some examples of high-yield hospital bonds:

- 14.875 percent Cuyahoga County, Ohio, Mount Sinai Medical Center bonds, maturing on December 1, 2014, rated A−
- 15.50 percent Sandusky County, Ohio, Memorial Hospital bonds, maturing on December 1, 2011, rated BBB+
- 14.75 percent Hospital Authority of Philadelphia bonds, maturing on April 1, 2010, rated A−

Notice that each of these high-yield bonds has a very far-off maturity date, around thirty years from now. These bonds, therefore, demonstrate the general rule: the longer the maturity term, the higher the yield. These examples also point out that the lower the credit rating is, the higher the yield will be. This means you must seriously consider the chance of increased risk of default.

Other high-yield revenue bonds include the following:

- 14.625 percent Texas Municipal Power Agency bonds, maturing on September 1, 2012, rated A+
- 13.50 percent Dallas–Fort Worth Regional Airport bonds, maturing on November 1, 2012, rated A
- 13.625 percent New York State Housing Finance Agency bonds (State University), maturing on May 1, 2012, rated AA−

Example: Investing for High Yield

Mildred Hartman of Boston, a recent widow, sold her late husband's highly successful computer company for a small fortune. She was worried over the amount of income she might gain from investing the proceeds from the sale of her husband's estate. Her broker said he could get her a high 16 percent tax-free return if she would invest in a municipal bond to be issued to enable a new electronics company on Route 128 to move into a factory building.

She was reluctant to put much of her money into municipal industrial development bonds because she thought (perhaps correctly) that there was a good deal of risk involved. She therefore decided to keep most of her husband's stocks and keep his estate in the bank savings account and Treasury bonds he had bought. Together these investments were earning 5 percent. However, she did invest some of her money in the municipal industrial revenue bonds at her adviser's suggestion.

By 1983, interest rates had dramatically fallen, but Mrs. Hartman was delighted to discover that her reluctant investment in the tax-free bonds had become seven times more profitable than her taxed earnings in the savings account and from the government bonds, both of which earned only 2¼ percent after all taxes.

In summary, if you wish to attain the highest yield, focus on hospital bonds, industrial bonds, or special-project revenue bonds. But be aware that these are riskier bonds, longer-maturing bonds, and frequently bonds that are less marketable and less liquid.

Example: Risk from Investing for High Yield

Fred Hopkins, a dentist in Chicago, invested $50,000 in municipal bonds issued for the Calumet Skyway Tollroad to construct a throughway near his home. "I figured it would be a quick route into the city that would cut down the driving time of commuters considerably and would therefore be a very successful venture. How could it fail to be a sound investment? It failed within one year after I bought the bonds."

What happened was typical of what can happen to unlucky bondholders in various municipal bond defaults when a toll bridge, road, hospital, or other new facility is built near a free federal or state highway, bridge, hospital, or other facility that drains away most of the potential paying customers.

INVESTING FOR SAFETY

If you prefer to obtain tax-exempt income with little or no risk at all on your bond investment, you should consider municipal securities directly backed or guaranteed by the federal government. You can be almost certain that these bonds will not go into default, but they pay a much lower yield than the hospital or revenue bonds discussed above. Among these types of safe securities are project notes backed by the federal government. Because project notes have short maturities, you will take only a minimum risk of loss due to interest rate fluctuation or inflationary erosion. Here are two examples of high-yield project notes:

- 7.77 percent Interregional Project note of Alaska, maturing in less than one year
- 7.60 percent Newark urban redevelopment note, maturing in nine months

As you can see, the interest on these federally guaranteed tax-free project notes is only about half of what you would receive on long-term bonds. When you invest in these two notes, you sacrifice a certain amount of yield in return for the guarantee of repayment by the U.S. government in the last resort. This guarantee will cost you more than other government-backed project notes issued from remote areas that pay a great deal more in yield for only a slightly longer maturity than one year. For example, in 1981– 82 when they were near their all-time high, govern- ment-guaranteed project notes *longer* than one year were available. Two examples follow:

- 9.04 percent Oklahoma City project notes, ma- turing in thirteen months
- 9.11 percent Youngstown, Ohio, project notes, maturing in fifteen months

The range in the coupon rates of project notes is due mostly to the current bond market conditions, the different lengths of maturity of the notes, famil- iarity of the name of the note issuer, and the re- moteness of the project's location.

Example: Risk-Free Investing

Carl Davenport was acutely safety conscious because his father had gone bankrupt and lost the family business. The first thing he asked his broker was this: "Can you find me bonds that are *absolutely* secure?" The broker could offer him three different types of secure tax-free bonds: (1) U.S. government–guaran- teed notes, with a maturity of only six months; (2) tax-free bonds insured by four different companies (but with thirty-year maturities); or (3) tax-free bonds backed by a bank letter of credit for ten years. All three types of securities have a triple A rating.

"Which of these three types of bonds is safest?" Davenport asked.

"The U.S. project notes are safest," replied the broker, "for they have the federal government's guarantee and are subject to the least fluctuation in price because of their very short maturity. The next safest are the insured bonds. These bonds lock up a long-term tax-free yield and are considered quite secure because the insurance companies will make your interest and principal payments to you if the municipality should go bankrupt or default on its payment to you."

Carl Davenport thought thirty years was too long a maturity for these insured bonds because the insurance protected him only against the bond's default, *not* against a drop in the bond's market resale value over the next thirty years. "What about the security of those ten-year bonds backed by a bank's letter of credit?" he said. "How safe are they?"

The broker responded, "Some bonds are backed unconditionally by major banks that themselves have triple A ratings. They are as secure as the bank itself."

"But how secure is that in case of a bankruptcy," Davenport pressed?

"Usually they are very safe," the broker replied. "But some banks do get downgraded in rating from triple A to double A, and that can affect the price of your bonds if you have to resell them. And some bank letters of credit are granted only on the condition that the municipality keep up to certain financial standards, so you do have to find out what the bank letter of credit actually guarantees."

"I'll buy the U.S. government project notes," the conservative Davenport decided. "They're the most secure tax-free investments of all."

Together, these insured and credit-enhanced bonds are the fastest-growing sector of the tax-free bond market because investors increasingly desire safety in an era of uncertainty.

INVESTING FOR PROTECTION AGAINST INTEREST RATE CHANGES

When the prevailing market rates of interest *rise*, the dollar or market value of all existing tax-free bonds with fixed rates of interest *fall*. In fact, the value of all fixed-rate securities, including all U.S. government and all corporate securities, suffers a decline when interest rates rise. Long-term securities fall the farthest and lose the most value.

If you are concerned that your long-term bonds will lose value if you decide to sell them before maturity, you might do better to concentrate on shorter-term bonds or short-term securities such as municipal notes and tax-free municipal commercial paper. You can purchase these municipal short-term securities for exactly the length of maturity that you wish—almost to the day. As with most other bonds, the interest rate of tax-exempt notes tends to reflect the length of maturity and the credit security of the issues.

Most tax-free short-term notes mature in ten to twelve months. But you can purchase three-month notes. Most tax-free municipal commercial paper contracts mature in only seven to ninety days (although they can be held for up to one year). By way of contrast, municipal bonds mature in three to forty years.

Interest-rate risk is a far more widespread problem than default risk for most investments, because interest-rate changes are very common whereas defaults and bankruptcies of municipalities are rare. With a few types of bonds you may face a serious risk of losing all your money in a bankruptcy, but you always face a serious danger of a decline in the value of your long-term bonds due to rises in interest rates or inflation rates or changes in U.S. government monetary policy.

However, don't choose tax-free short-term notes instead of long-term bonds blindly without regard for credit risk simply to protect yourself against the increased danger of interest-rate fluctuations on your long-term bonds' values. You should be aware that, in terms of credit security, the different types of tax-exempt notes range from the safest U.S.-guaranteed project notes, which offer the lowest yields, all the way to the riskiest tax-free notes for projects that may never be completed but that may offer you the very highest yields.

Variable-rate bonds provide one alternative to long-terms bonds that decrease in value due to interest-rate changes.

The volume of variable-rate securities of all kinds has grown very rapidly because of investors' concern about getting burned by holding bonds having long-term fixed-interest rates for thirty years. These variable-rate securities automatically adjust their interest rate every six months or yearly, according to the interest rate prevailing in the market on U.S. government Treasury bills, bonds, notes, or some other index. Thus your bond's variable rate of return is pegged to a changing current index, so it should never fall too far below its original market value.

Unlike these variable-rate securities, put bonds are

long-term bonds that have a fixed rate of interest, but they provide you, the investor, with the option to "put," or sell back, these bonds to the bond issuer at par—the full face value printed on the bonds—after three years or more. Thus, your thirty-year put bond is simultaneously a long-term bond, with the advantage to you of locking up a higher rate of long-term interest. At the same time it is a short-term bond of only three or so years, which protects you against the risk of long-term rises in interest rates if you do decide to put or sell your bond back to the issuer after a short time. Because put bonds are simultaneously long-term and short-term securities, their yield or rate of return tends to be higher than that of short-term bonds but lower than that of long-term bonds.

Put bonds, like variable-rate bonds, tend *not* to decline very much as interest rates rise, simply because you can always sell back your put bond to the bond issuer in three or so years at par value.

HOW TO ACHIEVE YOUR INVESTMENT OBJECTIVES

You can achieve your investment objectives in a variety of ways, one of which may be more to your liking than another.

For example, older persons might prefer to buy long-term bonds that offer a high yield for their children to inherit, or they might choose heavily discounted bonds that will steadily appreciate to par and offer their children or grandchildren capital gains as well as tax-free income. Some individuals might want to purchase a variety of very high-yielding defaulted bonds or other very high-risk securities. Remember that if a municipality defaults or goes bankrupt, you can deduct the loss on your tax return so that the government is, in effect, sharing a portion of your investment risk when you invest in risky securities.

CONSOLIDATE

You might want to diversify by purchasing a wide variety of very different types of bonds. Diversification as an investment strategy is well known in the stock market and is based on the simple principal that you do not put all your eggs in one basket but spread out your risk by purchasing a variety of several different stocks.

Municipal bonds are different from stocks in several important respects, however, and so your investment strategy must also be different. If you invest $10,000 in different stocks, for example, you can obtain adequate diversification of a stock portfolio. With municipal bonds, however, you would have to purchase $100,000 worth or more to achieve comparable diversification (unless you invest in bond funds or unit trusts). Municipal bonds are usually sold in denominations of $5,000, so your purchase of twenty different bonds could cost you $100,000. But does such diversification make sense? Not usually. What you should keep in mind is that twenty very small so-called odd lots of bonds might have to be sold for up to 5 percentage points less than a round lot of twenty-five bonds. As a result, most investors with limited means prefer to concentrate on only one bond or on a few bond issues. They would have to pay a penalty if they were forced to sell odd lots, and they want to avoid that eventuality. If you make a careful credit analysis on the bonds you are thinking of buying, you can eliminate much of the danger of default.

CHOOSING YOUR BONDS' MATURITY RANGE

One investor might prefer to invest *only* in long-term bonds, another investor *only* in very short-term notes. You can concentrate your purchases in one of these two different maturity ranges or any year in between. Your decision will depend on your view of risks and your view of good rates of return. If you need liquidity, you might take a compromise course and do two things: (1) put some money in long-term securities to take advantage of an attractive return, and (2) acquire some shorter-term bonds or notes as well. You can invest the proceeds of these shorter-term bonds or notes in currently profitable issues.

There are many ways to build a portfolio, but it is very important to remember that your investment plan, after you have purchased municipal bonds, should not be inflexible. Your circumstances may change, the market may change, your portfolio objectives may change. You must be able to adjust to these conditions either by swapping bonds or by selling them outright and purchasing others.

WHAT TO LEARN BEFORE BUYING A NEW BOND ISSUE

Because the municipal bond market is competitive, you should always determine how competitive the price of the bond you are being offered is. Ask your broker several questions before you buy. For starters, find out the difference between the winning bid and the second bid made by the various underwriters (known as the "cover").

If the cover was close, the professionals agreed on the value of the bonds. If the cover was wide, the second bid was quite different from the winning bid, and the market professionals expect that the selling price might have to be adjusted so that the underwriters can dispose of the bonds. Some professionals say that a wide cover is anything more than ten basis points (.10).

Next, try to find out the number of bonds that remain unsold. This is called the balance. If there is a large unsold balance, the bond issue is not selling well, and its price probably will soon be lowered so that the bonds can be sold off as soon as possible (unless the market improves).

Then, you might ask your broker why the bonds are selling at a higher or lower yield than similar bonds did a week earlier. If bonds sold the week before were not received well, they probably were overpriced; therefore, currently issued bonds should be offered at lower prices. Alternatively, if bonds offered earlier sold out immediately, new issues will probably be offered at a higher price.

At this point, it would be a good idea to find out if the market is getting stronger or weaker. If the market really is becoming stronger, you are justified in paying a higher price and therefore accepting a lower yield. But if the market is becoming weaker, you can hold out for a higher yield and obtain the same bonds for a lower price.

Last, you might find out what similar bonds are being offered in the secondary market—that is, as opposed to new issues.

Bonds very similar to those you are considering may be available at lower prices because, for example, a dealer may want to clear them out to avoid the cost of carrying them any longer.

HOW TO RESELL
YOUR BONDS

One of the greatest problems of buying tax-free bonds is that it can be difficult to resell them later. Many investors have to accept severely depressed prices for their bonds when they try to resell them. Bond dealers would typically offer only the lowest bargain-basement price for one or a few bonds. And dealers might even refuse to make a bid on bonds from a very small or obscure municipal issuer.

The stories are legion of investors who felt "taken to the cleaners," "robbed," or "insulted" by the drastically depressed prices they were forced to accept for their old bonds when they had to sell them off to a bond dealer.

Be aware that sometimes the best way to sell a bond is to direct a dealer firm to put the bond out for a bid with a municipal bond broker.

Municipal bond brokers restrict their clientele to bond dealers or dealer banks. That is why many investors have never heard about these brokers. Most investors are not even aware that they can get the same advantages of professional competition as a dealer can.

You can't call a broker's broker directly and ask him or her to put out your bonds for the bid, but you *can* tell your securities dealer to ask bond brokers to obtain bids. You simply say to your dealer, "Put my bonds out with a broker." You gain two advantages by selling your bonds this way: (1) you will be certain that many market professionals will see your bonds and, (2) you will know that you have probably obtained the best bid possible for your bonds in the current market.

Let me explain how this works. If you direct a securities firm to give your bonds to a broker's broker, your securities dealer will tell the broker's broker to put the bonds out for a bid. The broker's broker has a computer system with terminals on the trading desks of hundreds of other broker's dealers and dealer banks throughout the country. A description of your bonds will be transmitted immediately and printed out on those terminals. In addition, the broker's sales staff will call dealers whom they believe to have a special interest in your type of bond to ascertain if they want to bid for it.

Dealers will bid on your bonds for two reasons: (1) to acquire bonds for subsequent resale, and (2) to fulfill a specific order from a customer who will buy your bonds.

The broker's broker will tally the bids and report back to your dealer, who will then call you and tell you about the best bid. At this point you should ask your dealer what the second best bid, "the cover," was. You can then decide whether or not to sell the bonds. In essence you will have shown your bonds to a large number of the dealers.

HOW TO INVEST IN MUNICIPAL BONDS

In each year from 1981 to 1983, individual investors purchased over 75 percent of all new issues of municipals. Since over $125 billion tax-free long-term bonds and short-term notes were sold in 1982—it is clear that individual purchases of tax-exempt securities are huge.

The crucial shift occurred when individuals increased their purchases of municipal bonds tenfold between 1980 and 1981. At the same time, casualty insurance companies and banks cut their purchases of the bonds by more than half.

Some experts estimate that 18 million individual investors now own municipal bonds or shares in bond funds. It is easy to see why individuals account for the purchase of over 82 percent of the new issues offered in 1982–83. Obviously, as inflation has pushed salaries and the cost of living higher, more and more Americans have been elevated into higher tax brackets. Thus, each year a whole new group of wage earners confronts a higher tax charge for the same effective purchasing power. It is to these people that tax-free municipal bonds appeal most.

Although a large number of individuals purchase their bonds directly, many others depend on the help of managers of unit trusts, muncipal bond funds, trust accounts, investment advisory accounts, and other types of bond companies. All of these means of investment offer you certain advantages and disadvantages. Let us take a look at two of them.

UNIT TRUST FUNDS

In 1961 the Internal Revenue Service ruled that individual investors could purchase shares of municipal bonds from unit trust funds that would be tax free if two legal conditions were met: (1) the firms had to be operated as trusts, not as investment companies, and (2) the sponsors managing the fund had to hold the portfolios to maturity. Over the past twenty years, many major bond dealers and brokerage houses created unit trust funds. The buying professionals of these firms assembled the portfolio for the trustee. Municipal bond trusts usually hold fifteen to thirty different bond issues bought from one brokerage firm or a group of firms to meet specific requirements. One trust might hold only A-rated bonds, for example; another might specialize in bonds with a specified maturity date—or hospital bonds or bonds issued within one state. A typical unit trust fund manages only $50 million in assets. However, it should be understood that several dozen—and sometimes hundreds—of such funds are grouped under one firm or one group of many firms.

The minimum investment in most cases is $5,000

in unit trusts, with less required for additional commitments. Nevertheless, the typical purchaser acquires shares worth $20,000 to $25,000. Before you decide on a fund, you should evaluate the performance of different trust managements and obtain the answers to the following questions:

- What was the stated yield of the trust at the date of creation?
- How good is the performance of the sponsor's other unit trusts? What has their total return been over the years?
- How large a commission or fee will the sponsor charge me?
- What is the length of maturity of the bond portfolio?
- What credit criteria have the sponsors set for the bond portfolio? What is the actual credit rating of the worst bonds in the portfolio (in the absence of any credit rating on some bonds in the portfolio)?
- How many years will I hold the shares of a particular unit trust?
- What is the extent of specialization, diversity, and risk of the portfolio of the unit trust I am considering? Does it include, for example, different geographical areas or different categories of bonds?
- What are the unit trust manager's methods of calculating the redemption price, the price I will receive if I decide to cash in my shares of the unit trust before their maturity date?

Municipal bond trusts offer a simple and convenient way for you to invest in municipal bonds. Besides the attractions of tax-exempt income and professionally selected portfolios, they can offer the added safety of a diversified portfolio for an investment of as little as $1,000 in a few cases.

Municipal bond trusts are unit investment trusts that consist of fixed portfolios of municipal bonds that you keep until maturity (unless the bonds are called or sold before maturity). The trustees will send you monthly, quarterly, or semiannual checks, or you can reinvest interest and principal. As the bonds mature or are called, the principal is returned to you as a return of capital. Bonds may be sold out of the trust if the sponsors feel that holding them would endanger the interest of the unit holders. The proceeds would then be paid to the unit holders. A unit holder may incur a capital gain or loss when the trust disposes of a bond.

There are two general categories of municipal bond trusts: *general trusts* and *state trusts.* General trusts might include bonds from various states and territories; state trusts hold bonds from a single state only. State trusts provide income that may be free from state and local taxes in the issuing state, as well as from federal taxes. Individual investors have purchased over $45 billion of tax-free investment trusts. New varieties are being created continually.

MUNICIPAL BOND FUNDS

Since 1976 open-end bond funds have been established that are able to sell off old bonds and purchase new ones. This ability to trade bonds in the fund makes open-end funds different from municipal bond unit trusts, which cannot purchase new bonds to add to the trust. Open-end bond funds thereby have a good chance of avoiding the long-term consequences that continuing rises in interest rates can have on a rigid portfolio.

Investing in certain municipal bonds funds can pose problems, however, and you should be quite selective in which bond fund you choose.

You should be aware that the managers of bond funds charge a fee *each year* or about .7 percent of your total money invested to cover management fees and expenses. Purchasing shares in a bond fund will cost you somewhat more over the long haul of ten, fifteen, or twenty years than buying the bonds yourself. These bond fund management fees and charges are "operating costs," which you pay indirectly in the form of a lower annual return.

Should you invest directly in bonds on your own *or* invest in a bond fund? The answer depends on whether you want the convenience of having someone else do the work of choosing your bonds and keeping your records for you. The main thing that bond funds offer you is their ability as bond traders—indeed as predictors of interest rates. However, many experts doubt that interest rates can be forecast.

Bond fund managers will argue that their trading ability is very valuable because they can trade bonds to get the fund's portfolio out of bad bonds and into better ones. However, the track record of a number of funds until 1982 was poor. Part of the problem is that when it sells municipal bonds, the bond fund frequently incurs a loss. Therefore, unless the portfolio manager is *extremely* skillful, the more bonds the fund sells, the more losses it is likely to incur.

On the plus side, bond funds do offer you diversity because of the many bonds in the fund's port-folio. Bond funds also offer you a high degree of convenience because the fund managers handle all the details for you—purchasing the bonds, investigating the bonds, storing the bonds, clipping the coupons on the bonds, and other recordkeeping chores involved in buying bonds. Bond funds also make it easier for someone with a small amount of capital to enter the bond market. However, the bond funds' primary claim that they provide professional management that can successfully trade bonds to increase your earnings has not been fully borne out by every bond funds' performance since they were first established in 1976. Only certain funds excelled.

In short, my study shows most bond funds make money when interest rates are coming down, and many of them lose money or barely break even when interest rates are going up.

Some bond funds are far better managed than the others and have consistently earned a fairly hefty total rate of return—without taking too much risk. So, make sure to compare the funds before you invest and choose a bond fund which has a fairly good track record. Both *Forbes* Magazine and the *Lipper Analytical Service* regularly publish rankings of all the municipal bond funds—long term, short term, high yield, in-state, insured, etc. Make sure to check both these rankings for they use different criteria. *Forbes* ranks the funds according to their current yield, but *Lipper* ranks funds by their more comprehensive total rate of return; which measures not only your current yield but also whether your asset principal investment in the fund has declined or risen in its value.

You should note that because bond fund managers are aware that it is difficult to predict market conditions, they tend to follow the leader. That is, when only a limited number of "name" bonds are available in sufficient volume with solid credit and high performance, a large number of managers flock to buy them up, but then rush to sell them all at once if the bonds decline in value. Naturally, this practice can cause the prices of the bonds to fluctuate.

Individual investors have purchased over $40 billion of tax-free bond funds. There are long term bond funds, intermediate-term bond funds, short-term bond funds, tax-free money market bond funds, and insured bond funds. There are also tax-free bond funds that invest only in bonds of a single state for those investors who want triple tax exemption.

Most Bond Funds are sold by companies that offer a so-called "family of different kinds of funds" so that you can shift from a short-term fund to a long-term fund on any day without charge (or a nominal charge).

Be aware that sometimes certain bond funds invest some of their money in taxable U.S. government securities or taxable corporate bonds so that you may have to pay some tax on your "tax-free bond fund." You should also check carefully for the so-called expense ratio for your bond fund to see how high the management fees and other expenses are. The bigger and older bond funds usually have lower expense ratios. Anything more than .8 percent ratio is considered high.

DIRECT INVESTMENT

Like many individual investors, you may choose to buy new-issue bonds directly rather than through a fund. It is clear that during the past decade you would have been better off buying municipal bonds on your own. At the same time, however, you could incur greater risk than you wish to take if you invest on your own.

But are you assured of higher safety in a bond fund? Not necessarily. This is due to the fact that many funds have been induced to include certain higher-risk issues in their portfolios—bonds rated A– or unrated—in order to increase the yield of the whole fund. Some funds stretch for the highest possible yields that high-risk issues return in order to compete with other funds and new funds, and to appeal to investors. You could also lose from investing in certain bond funds because they are tied up in very long-term bond issues, making yourself vulnerable to the adverse effects of inflation and changing interest rates. In conclusion, you probably can earn a higher overall return, limit risk, and maintain liquidity if you invest on your own. Nevertheless, many investors will still prefer the convenience of a bond fund.

6

STRATEGIES FOR INVESTING IN MUNICIPAL BONDS

J. P. Morgan advised young investors to buy when everyone else wanted to sell and to sell when everyone else wanted to buy. To the extent that the bond market is a buyers' and sellers' market, it is true that you should wait for a large number of sellers to materialize before you buy bonds, and you should wait until many buyers are available before you sell bonds.

But how do you know when there is a glut or a scarcity of bonds for sale? How do you determine when bonds might increase or decrease in value? A number of indicators will help you predict bond performance. Among those general economic conditions that are *most* favorable to purchasing bonds are:

- Declining current rates of inflation
- Declining interest rates
- Stable money supply
- Flexible Federal Reserve policy
- Limited federal government demand for money
- Limited corporate demand for money

In order to develop the best investment strategy in municipals, you should consider the following specific bond market indicators. I will list these four indicators and then explain, in detail, why each is important to you.

- The ratio reflecting the percent of return on tax-exempt as opposed to taxable securities
- The Delphis Hanover range of yield curve scales
- *The Bond Buyer*'s placement ratio
- The par value of Blue List offerings and the thirty-day visible supply.

THE RATIO OF TAX-EXEMPT
TO TAXABLE SECURITIES

This ratio of tax-exempt security yields to the yields of taxable bonds (the municipals/government ratio) is the most important of all the ratios we will consider. This ratio tells you exactly what percentage tax-exempt bonds are paying, at the moment, in relation to the safest taxable yield.

Over many decades this ratio of municipals/government or tax-exempt/taxable bonds has been plotted in order to help professional municipal bond investors determine the best time and the worst time to invest. To obtain this ratio, you can simply ask any broker, or alternatively, you can divide the current rate of return on any tax-exempt twenty-five-year AAA state bond by the current return on a twenty-five-year U.S. bond that is taxed at the federal level:

$$\frac{\text{AAA MUNICIPAL BOND}}{\text{U.S. GOVERNMENT BOND}} = X\%$$

As you will see from the graph on page 74 provided by Merrill Lynch, changes have been plotted in the relationship between municipals and government bonds over the years. There are peaks when investors have received more and valleys when investors have received less rate of return by buying municipals than by buying taxable U.S. government securities.

At certain times, as you see from the peaks on the graph—as in 1969, for example, when the municipals/government ratio reached over 93 percent and approached its all-time high—the investor was overcompensated for buying a tax-exempt bond instead of a taxable security. These are often exceptionally good times to buy municipal bonds.

Generally speaking, given a ratio of 72 percent as the long-run average over the years of this municipals/government ratio or tax-exempt/taxable bond ratio, if the ratio goes above that 72 percent and reaches 80 percent or more, you would gain a considerable comparative advantage by choosing tax-free over taxable securities at that particular moment in time. Thus you should consider investing in municipal tax-exempt securities when that ratio rises above 80 percent. Likewise, given the same long-run average, when the ratio falls below 65 percent, it is not usually a good time to invest in municipals, for you would be undercompensated for your investment in tax-exempt securities. At such times you should probably invest either in taxable securities, in very short-term tax-exempt securities or tax-exempt money

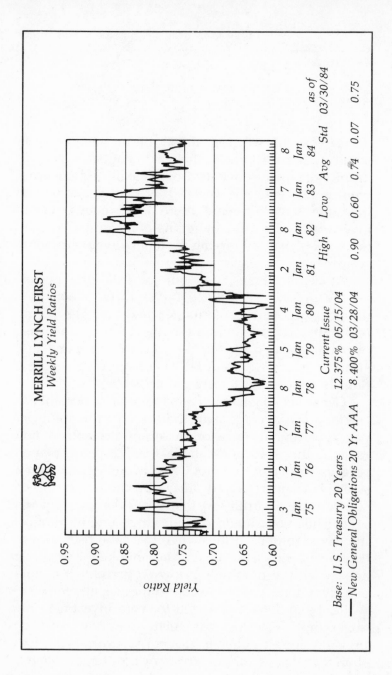

MERRILL LYNCH FIRST
Weekly Yield Ratios

Yield Ratio

0.95
0.90
0.85
0.80
0.75
0.70
0.65
0.60

3
Jan
75

2
Jan
76

7
Jan
77

8
Jan
78

5
Jan
79

4
Jan
80

2
Jan
81

8
Jan
82

7
Jan
83

8
Jan
84

Current Issue

12.375% 05/15/04

8.400% 03/28/04

High   Low   Avg   Std   as of
                              03/30/84

0.90   0.60   0.74   0.07   0.75

Base: U.S. Treasury 20 Years
— New General Obligations 20 Yr AAA

funds, or in very deep-discount bonds where you may be adequately rewarded.

The municipals/government ratio gives a good indication of the value of bonds over short periods of time, but it does not tell you if interest rates are going to rise or fall over long intervals. In other words, the ratio shows only the current relative value of tax-exempt bonds in comparison to taxable bonds. It does not reveal the future value of your bonds. The ratio is very important to consider, but you could get hurt if you invest solely on this basis, especially at times when interest rates are rising substantially.

THE DELPHIS HANOVER YIELD CURVES

A series of yields for a bond issue, with serial maturities over a number of consecutive years, is referred to as a yield curve or scale. Delphis Hanover Corporation publishes yield curve scales that give you the yields, or rates of return, on average bonds of each type. This range of yield curve scales will help you to know where you are being offered a bond in relation to the overall market. If the bond you are shown is substantially out of line with the Delphis Hanover yield curve, you should seek an explanation from your investment advisor before you invest. However, if the bond has a higher yield than the curve, it may well be a bargain.

Each Delphis Hanover yield curve scale is a matrix of actual bond prices and yields. It shows the acceptance levels and price changes, by maturity and by credit ratings, derived daily from both the primary and secondary municipal markets.

RANGE OF YIELD CURVE SCALES

The range of yield curve scales show where the municipal market is at the close of every day (or week). They enable you to see at a glance the yield-spread relationship between each maturity and each grade of bond. This is of enormous help to you in your buying, selling, and swapping decisions.

These scales are also useful for spotting market trends, formulating market timing and strategy, picking the most attractive yield for a bond that meets your investment objectives, and avoiding certain bonds that may be overpriced in relation to the market.

THE PLACEMENT RATIO

The placement ratio is published weekly in *The Bond Buyer*, the major newspaper of municipal bond market professionals. This placement ratio indicates how well new bond issues are selling, as compared to bonds already issued. If the ratio is low, that means the new bond issues are not selling well. The "overhang" of the new bonds in the hands of the dealers may result in price reductions—a possible bargain for you.

You should be aware of the fact that there are *two* placement ratios: the *overall ratio* and the *competitive ratio*. The overall ratio indicates how many bonds have

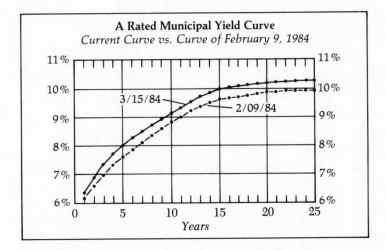

A Rated Municipal Yield Curve
Current Curve vs. Curve of February 9, 1984

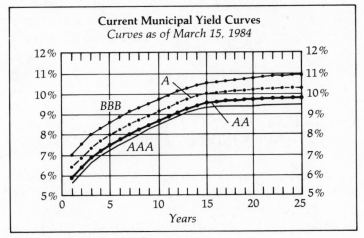

Current Municipal Yield Curves
Curves as of March 15, 1984

Data Sources: Delphis Hanover Corp.

been sold for all new issues. It is more indicative of market performance than the competitive placement ratio, which measures only the sale of issues that are put on the market after competitive bidding.

If buyers are not taking a large portion of the new issues at current offering prices, the underwriters may have to reduce the prices of the remaining bonds to meet the market. Often this competitive placement ratio, therefore, will indicate periods in which the whole municipal bond market is suffering from congestion and possible overpricing. It is conceivable that underwriters will reduce the prices of bonds they hold during such times, thus resulting in a greater yield in the immediate future.

You should consider the overall and the competitive ratios together. Either one, taken by itself, can give you a distorted picture of the market. You should also study the potential supply of new bonds that may be offered on the market during the next thirty days (the thirty-day visible supply) and the size of the Blue List, discussed below.

THE BLUE LIST AND THE THIRTY-DAY VISIBLE SUPPLY

The Blue List, so called because it is published daily on blue paper, presents bonds that are offered for sale. It does not give a complete listing, however. Dealers might not report issues that have not been selling well or bonds that they are holding back from the market. Also, dealers who have taken bonds out of a new issue for their secondary accounts will report only a portion of the bonds they own. A knowledgeable investor will ask a dealer, "Do you have any bonds behind your offering?" If the dealer does have a large number of bonds and is eager to sell them, you might find a bargain. The Blue List provides a list of the prices at which the seller is offering the bonds. There is no guarantee that the seller will get this price. Investors often confuse stock market tables that print actual traded prices with the Blue List prices which are more of a desired price. The size of the Blue List, however, can be used to determine the changing pattern of supply—approximately. The size of the current Blue List is published weekly in *The Bond Buyer's Credit Markets.*

The thirty-day visible supply of new bond issues is another index of the relative supply of bonds on or coming on the market. An influx of new bonds totaling over $2 or $3 billion may well signal that there are going to be some real bargains available. This huge oversupply, or glut, of new bonds must compete for buyer interest, and so there will be strong pressure to offer some extra yield incentive. This thirty-day visible supply figure is also published weekly in *The Bond Buyer's Credit Markets.*

TRENDS IN MUNICIPAL BOND MARKETS FOLLOW THE U.S. SECURITIES

The prices and yields of municipal bonds tend to follow the changes in U.S. government bonds. As the market in taxable bonds, such as government bonds and notes, changes, the market in municipal bonds is also likely to change in the same direction.

The thirty-day U.S. government bond index will indicate the changes in those bonds that usually cause similar changes in the rates on municipal bonds, especially dollar bonds.

Municipal bond dealers and underwriters usually follow the interest rates on government issues throughout the day. This is significant because rates on taxed bonds (such as U.S. government bonds, bills, notes, federal agency securities, and even corporate bonds) usually affect the interest you receive from municipal bonds. Their trends are very closely related.

OTHER FACTORS
AFFECTING BOND RATES

Professional investors watch the rate of return at which the very strongest-rated (AAA) general obligations are being sold on the bond market. Often the yields of new high-quality AAA general-obligation bonds stand as an indicator of the true strength of the current bond market. As a result, the rates that are gained for these new AAA bonds will affect the yields of bonds carrying a lower rating. It is believed that all other municipal securities tend to "trade off" those state names that bear a AAA rating, which, incidentally, tend to be state names. You should watch the interest that AAA bonds return to determine the price and interest you can and should expect from bonds with comparable or lower ratings.

Thus, bonds rated BAA will return a lesser relative rate of interest than AAA bonds when the market for AAA bonds is rising, and a higher relative rate when it is falling. The lower-rated bonds are much more volatile than the bonds with the highest rating. The trick is to determine whether the market is rising or falling—and trade accordingly.

To summarize, before you buy or sell bonds, you should take five steps: (1) determine current inflation and interest rates, (2) find the ratio of tax-exempt to taxable bonds available, (3) learn the price and yield of the particular bond you are interested in, (4) compare your bond to the rest of the market according to the Delphis Hanover range of yield curve scales, and (5) consult the Blue List and *The Bond Buyer* to see how the new issues are selling.

Does this sound complicated? It is not. These five indicators are printed in the weekly *Bond Buyer*. You simply look them up for that week. You must consider all of these indicators *together* in order to anticipate the direction of the bond index—at least with some certainty.

CONSTRAINTS ON BUYING BONDS

The municipal bond market is an extremely segmented and compartmentalized marketplace that places a wide variety of constraints on individual and institutional investors. Most individuals buy bonds only in their own state because they seek double or triple tax exemption. Most institutions, like bank trust departments, are constrained by law as to what types of bonds they can and cannot invest in. For example, they can invest only in "investment-grade" bonds that are rated Baa or better. Most small issues of bonds are sold by municipalities *only* to local investors; they are not available to other buyers. In short, the municipal market is very fragmented by very particular buyers, legal constraints, and geographic considerations.

The average municipal bond interest rate is not determined on a unified national basis, but instead often differs greatly from one region to another.

Another municipal bond market constraint arises from personal foibles. Some investors restrict their purchase of bonds for purely emotional reasons, resulting perhaps, in long-term loss. Some banks, institutions, and individuals prefer to buy bonds in local companies or municipalities that they feel they understand and with which they are familiar. The bond market overall may be operated on the principal of supply and demand, but sometimes it is affected by personal predictions.

CHAPTER
7

INDIVIDUAL RISKS OF HOLDING MUNICIPAL BONDS

Recession, cuts in federal spending, widespread taxpayer dissatisfaction, high interest rates, inflation, defaults, and near defaults on municipal bonds between 1973 and 1983 have made many of us well aware that investment in municipal bonds can be risky. The four most common risks that face municipal bond investors are:

- Default
- Loss of asset value
- Loss of liquidity
- Reduction in credit rating

The risk of *default* arises if a municipality goes bankrupt and cannot pay the interest or principal on its bonds. This is the most serious risk because if default occurs, you could lose all of your investment and income. However, this is a very rare event.

Loss of asset value is caused when interest rates increase. As rates rise, bond prices fall. This is a risk that all fixed return investments must face regardless of the quality of the investment.

Loss of liquidity occurs when market conditions deteriorate as investors of all types transfer their funds to more profitable ventures. You suddenly might find that there are few buyers for your bonds. Thus if you need to obtain cash to switch to more lucrative investments yourself, you might have to take a substantial loss on your bonds.

Reduction in credit rating is brought about when the rating services see that a municipality or bond-issuing authority is facing a fiscal problem and therefore may have difficulty meeting its bond obligations The rating services may then lower the municipality's rating. When that happens, the value of the city's bonds decreases.

A number of bond analysts believe that investors now have to face greater danger in the bond market than they have had to at any time since the Great Depression. Partly, this could be because of downgradings of many municipalities' credit ratings; the shift away from GO bonds backed by taxes; and the predominance of unsophisticated buyers in today's bond market.

If several major defaults were to occur, buyers of municipal bonds might stop buying bonds of many other municipalities.

This in turn would make it difficult for many municipalities and other public authorities to raise money to meet current expenses.

STRATEGIES FOR
COPING WITH RISKS

It is a fact of financial life that when you invest in most municipal bonds you run a certain amount of risk, no matter how careful you are. Here are some strategies for minimizing your risks:

- If the bond market is declining very rapidly, avoid the bond market entirely; invest instead in non-fixed-income securities or money market funds.
- If the bond market is declining steadily but not collapsing, buy only very short-term securities that you can more readily hold to maturity.
- Buy only the highest-quality bonds, especially those guaranteed by state and the federal governments or those backed by an assured source of funding like insured bonds or bonds backed by a bank letter of credit.
- Avoid bonds issued to fund potentially unsound projects such as unneeded hospitals and toll roads and tunnels to be built near toll-free facilities.
- Be especially wary of bonds issued by states or cities that are heavily dependent on federal revenue sharing. Be careful about investing in start-up projects if the municipality has *no* experience in doing them.

Of course, your own personal views of the risks of different types of bonds can affect your investment strategy. Thus, if you are *extremely* wary of risk, invest only in *insured* bonds or bonds or notes *guaranteed* by the U.S. government. If you are concerned about marketability and liquidity, you would probably prefer short-term bonds or notes with a high rating. If you are worried about adverse economic conditions in certain parts of the country, such as Detroit or the Northeast, you might consider investing in the strongest regions of the Sunbelt. If you do not want to risk investing in industrial-revenue bonds of unstable industries such as automobiles or steel, you might consider investing in those bonds issued in connection with the new technology industries.

If you believe that the nation's economic condition will improve, you might buy long-term bonds with a discount price of between 55 and 65 percent in anticipation of good capital appreciation. Finally, if you think the economy is in a recession and suffering inflation ("stagflation"), nationally and worldwide, and that these conditions will persist, you should think about buying only high-quality short-term bonds, notes, or put bonds (discussed on p. 100). They are safer, depreciate slowly in a bad market, and appreciate more rapidly in a good market.

RISK OF TAXPAYERS' REVOLTS

The municipal bond market, and its investors, can be adversely affected by events not caused by economic conditions. One noteworthy example was the passage of Proposition 13 in California. This was brought about not by any financial crisis, but by the political antagonism of California voters toward high state and municipal taxes, lavish spending, and excessive debt.

That bill and later acts restricted the extent to which state and local governments could spend, tax, and issue bonds. Also, all government budgets were required to be balanced.

To varying degrees, forty-six other states have experienced taxpayers' revolts similar to the Proposition 13 movement in California. Disgruntled voters throughout the nation have passed an array of new laws that put state limits on public taxing powers and municipal spending powers and severely limit the ability of states and municipalities to issue new bonds. As an individual investor, you should be very careful to avoid buying bonds of municipalities that are experiencing such taxpayers' revolts unless you are very familiar with that municipality's finances and tax laws. Ask your broker about such dangers for each bond or note that you consider buying.

RISK OF BAD MUNICIPAL ACCOUNTING

Certainly the technical default and the near collapse of New York City in 1974–75 financially affected the entire Northeast and most of the U.S. municipal bond market. This crisis was not directly caused by inflation, high interest rates, or depression. It was the result of the city's inadequate accounting and reporting practices. In 1975 New York City's books suposedly were balanced in accordance with the city's financial practices. Actually, the city had accumulated a hidden deficit of close to $5 billion. The shortcomings in the methods of New York City's accounting disclosure affected the entire bond market because investors became convinced that they could not get a clear or easily comprehensible picture of any municipality's finances. Naturally, for a period, a number of investors were reluctant to buy municipal bonds. Bond issuers were therefore forced to offer bonds at higher yields. The New York City crisis led to many beneficial accounting reforms across the country among the whole range of municipalities. However, some communities still have poor accounting.

RISK OF CALL

Investors also run a risk brought about by fluctuating national and international interest rates. For example, if interest rates fall, municipalities may call in bonds sold earlier at high rates of interest and issue new bonds at a lower interest rate. If your bonds are called, you will not earn the high yield you hoped for. Instead, you may be forced to reinvest in bonds that offer less income. You thereby lose some of the profit you anticipated. It is quite likely that governments will call in old, expensive bonds in the coming years because of the substantial drop in interest rates since 1982.

To protect yourself against the risk of a call, you might choose to invest only in non-callable bonds. Or you might purchase municipal securities with a call that is many years in the future. If you buy callable bonds, always judge that investment from the very outset as if you were definitely going to have all those bonds called on the *very first call date*. If your purchase of these bonds makes economic sense to you for that first date, then these bonds will pay a sufficient return to you for every subsequent call date. Before you purchase callable bonds, always ask your broker this question: "What will be my rate of return or yield to the *first call date?*" Do *not* count on the yield to the final maturity date printed on the bond.

8

SHORT-TERM MUNICIPAL SECURITIES

Inflation ravages the market for fixed-income securities, and especially the market for very long-term municipal bonds. When inflation and interest rates go up, as they did from 1970 to 1981, bond prices go down, and vice versa.

For example, IBM sold a debt issue of $1 billion at near par of $1,000 with a coupon yield of 8 percent, although the prime lending rate was already above 11 percent. Barely fourteen months later, that same bond had plummeted in value to $750 as the prime rate climbed to 21 percent. This was due to the fact that low-interest-coupon bonds are less attractive when new long-term bonds are being offered with coupon rates double or triple those of older bonds. As interest rates rise, the older low-interest-coupon bonds lose value until their price decline makes their yield, or rate of return, comparable to the rate on new bonds in the current market. Longer-term bonds will usually fall the farthest in price, and therefore their yields have been forced to rise the highest of any bonds.

However, the high interest rates that have prevailed since 1977 have also made it far more difficult for municipalities to afford to issue long-term bonds when they are required to pay rates of 10 percent to 15 percent. Consequently, they have expanded their offerings of short-term municipal notes to avoid locking themselves into these high rates for twenty or thirty years. These short-term notes and short-term bonds have become popular with investors because they can avoid the risks involved in tying up their money for long periods of time when interest rates are fluctuating wildly.

Municipalities offer a number of different types of short-term notes:

- Bond-anticipation notes
- Revenue-anticipation notes
- Tax-anticipation notes
- Tax-allocation notes
- General-obligation notes
- Project notes
- Municipal commercial paper

All of these short-term notes can be secured by certain sources of funds: future taxes; revenue from federal, state, or other sources; future bond issues; or bank letters of credit.

BOND-ANTICIPATION NOTES

Bond-anticipation notes (BANS) carry a higher risk than some other notes because they are not secured by specific taxes or other income; they are only as safe as the ability of a municipality to sell bonds in the future. Most are quite sound, but they are vulnerable to future increases in interest rates that might cause the issuing authority to hesitate to issue new bonds to redeem the old ones in a relatively short period of time. Bond anticipation notes are also vulnerable to other conditions such as a depressed bond market or periods when municipalities find it difficult to sell bonds because of a weakened credit rating resulting from a financial crisis within the municipality itself. New York City is an example of this. The credit security behind a city transit bond-anticipation note for the building of a new section of the subway system was placed in limbo when the funds for the entire project were suspended. The ability of the municipality to pledge its taxing power, if needed, to retire the notes can lessen the risk.

REVENUE-ANTICIPATION NOTES

Revenue-anticipation notes (RANS) are considered quite safe because they are secured by specific future revenues. Such revenues include funds that supposedly will be provided by federal and state legislation. RANS might become riskier in the future as a result of federal and state cutbacks in revenue-sharing programs.

For example, federal revenues for welfare have been severely slashed, affecting municipal welfare programs for the homeless, the old, the sick, the undernourished, and the jobless. Federal revenues for state and municipal education have been cut at all levels. Federal revenues for municipal and state environmental protection projects and expenditures have been drastically reduced. Revenue anticipation notes that were sold in anticipation that municipalities would be certain of receiving those federal and state monies in some cases have been affected by these delays and cutbacks in revenues. Nevertheless, despite these problems the vast majority of municipal revenue anticipation notes have been considered secure up to now because such RANS were issued only when specific state and/or federal revenues were explicitly designated for municipalities.

TAX-ANTICIPATION NOTES

Tax-anticipation notes (TANS) are also considered secure because they are backed by taxes on income, property, and sales. Since TANS are issued for periods of a year or less, an erosion of the tax base due to economic causes or taxpayers' revolts probably will not seriously affect them, for the tax measures are voted and approved before they are offered. Rapid or severe economic downturns, like the one Detroit experienced, could make TANS less attractive than they have been in the past, however. In 1982, for example, the City Council of Detroit voted a sharp increase in taxes in order to cover its soaring expenses. However, Detroit already had been forced to cut back on all public services because of its economic crisis during 1981–82 and loss of industry, plant closings, and massive layoffs of workers in the automotive industry. In this circumstance an investor considering tax-anticipation notes might be very worried about the ability of Detroit to raise the new tax revenues that the City Council has voted. Always ask yourself before you invest in tax-anticipation notes, "Do I feel totally confident that this municipality will collect these taxes?" Professional investors always try to determine what percentage of taxes will be uncollectable. Municipalities must record figures on previously uncollected taxes. You might also be concerned not simply about the *ability* of a municipality to pay its taxes but also about *willingness* of its citizens to pay their taxes. Taxpayers' revolts have exacerbated this concern among municipal bond investors. Despite these bondholder concerns, the vast majority of tax-anticipation notes are *not* vulnerable.

TAX-ALLOCATION NOTES

Tax-allocation notes pose a far more serious question for bond investors because they are backed by taxes that are to be specifically allocated from real estate assessments. The tax-allocation notes of California became infamous because they were strongly affected by Proposition 13 by which an overwhelming two-thirds of the voters put serious restraints on the future taxing power of the state. Holders of tax-allocation notes suffered severely because of the voters' sharp limit on future taxes and because Proposition 13 forced a rollback of the basis of property tax assessment to the 1976 level, thereby sharply cutting the state's taxable funds.

GENERAL-OBLIGATION NOTES

General-obligation notes are backed by the taxing power of the municipal authority, whether state, city, or municipality, and usually carry the same rating as its bonds, for they have available the same source of funds. However, general-obligation notes are not backed by specific taxes, revenues, or bonds. In other words, they are backed by the general sources of municipal funds, not by one specific source.

PROJECT NOTES

Project notes are the safest short-term municipal securities because they ultimately are backed by the federal government. They are also secured by the revenue the issuing authority anticipates it will collect from housing and urban renewal projects, which they are almost exclusively sold to finance. Project notes usually offer the lowest rate of return of any municipal note because they are generally regarded as virtually risk-free due to their backup credit support by the U.S. government. Because project notes usually set the lowest rate of return of any municipal notes, they provide a base or benchmark from which to judge the fairness of the rate of return of other tax-exempt notes.

MUNICIPAL COMMERCIAL PAPER

Municipal commercial paper consists of very short-term tax-exempt obligations covered by bank letters of credit. They are freely negotiable. They mature in less than a year; in fact, many of them mature in only fifteen to forty-five days. They are usually issued in very large denominations—sometimes as large as $1 million—but most of these notes are for $100,000. Paper units for $50,000 or $25,000 are rare but sometimes available. Municipal commercial paper is issued at low interest rates—3 to 8 percent—to meet transitory imbalances or cash shortages. Because commercial paper is sold in such large denominations, you can almost predetermine the day you want to redeem it.

Commercial paper is *unsecured* by specific municipal taxes, revenues, or future bond sale proceeds that back up other municipal short-term obligations. All *secured* debt must be paid first if a government goes bankrupt. If any assets are left, the commercial paper receives payment. You are really dependent on the municipality's ability to roll over or refinance your paper when it matures. You must ask your bond broker to check the *available revenue ratio* (published in the municipality's financial statements). This ratio tells how much cash or revenue the municipality can depend on to meet its obligations as opposed to how dependent it is on the banks for cash. The ratio ranges from .10 percent for a cash-short city to 1.30 percent for a city with an abundant cash flow.

Finally, because the legal and financial requirements that must be met vary from one state to another, only a few dealers have the capacity or inclination to deal in commercial paper. For you, as an investor, this means that there are only limited sources where you can buy or sell your holdings quickly.

Municipal commercial paper can be issued by many different types of municipalities and even by non-government bodies such as private universities. The University of Chicago, for example, can issue municipal commercial paper, but it will have to pay a higher rate of return than would the city of Chicago or the state of Illinois or some other sizable issuer with the ability to tax.

9

RECENT INNOVATIONS IN MUNICIPAL SECURITIES

Investors recently have been given the opportunity to buy bonds that offer new features geared toward coping with inflation and with sharply fluctuating interest rates. These include:

- Variable-term bonds
- Flexible-rate securities
- Put bonds
- Families of funds
- Bonds with warrants
- Zero-coupon bonds

VARIABLE-TERM BONDS AND OTHER FLEXIBLE-RATE SECURITIES

Variable-term bonds and other flexible-rate securities differ from other securities in that their interest rates vary as the interest rate on various federal government issues—the floating interest rate—changes. The rates are computed on the basis of average interest rates of federal government securities for the twenty-six weeks before interest is paid and distributed semiannually. The return on variable-rate bonds is usually lower than the interest paid on fixed-rate securities. Variable-rate bonds are usually traded at par. Because of their low interest and small discount, many professional and institutional investors avoid flexible-rate securities entirely.

PUT BONDS

Put bonds, first issued in 1980, offer a full sell-back provision, or "put," to appeal to investors who are reluctant to buy long-term bonds. Put bonds are sometimes called option bonds because they give you the option of selling the bonds back to the municipal issuer at face value at any time five years after they were issued, or you can hold the bond until its final maturity. Some bonds can be "put," or sold back, annually or semiannually, with thirty days' or only seven days' notice. That makes some of these put bonds equal to very short-term securities. Put bonds are frequently supported by a letter of credit guaranteeing that a bank or other financial institution will buy any bonds the trustees cannot redeem. Depending on the bank's own credit rating, these bonds can carry an AA or AAA rating.

FAMILIES OF FUNDS

Families of funds, i.e. open ended funds, have been organized to buy bonds of various kinds. The fund organizers offer them in groups, each of which includes one type of bond. They range from issues with a high risk and a high yield to those with a low risk and a low return. Investors have been attracted to them for two reasons: (1) they believe the funds let them take advantage of professional management, and (2) the families of funds allow the investors to switch from one fund in the family to another within twenty-four hours for any reason without incurring transaction costs.

Here is one example of how you might change from tax-exempt to non-exempt bonds within a family of funds. During the first quarter of 1980, when interest rates were at a peak of 20 percent, taxable bonds gave the highest yield available. However, interest rates plummeted to 11 percent in the second quarter of 1980. When that happened, you could have switched to a fund holding tax-exempt bonds at 8 percent. By doing so, you would have received a 6 percent capital gain per share from the fund on top of the 8 percent coupon yield because the prices of tax-exempt bonds rose in the quarter. The 6 percent capital gain was taxable, but when it was coupled with the 8 percent tax-exempt coupon, the combined income after tax would have been hard to beat if you had decided to keep your money in the taxable fund. Remember, however, that some families of funds impose a sales charge; others deduct fees before paying interest.

BONDS WITH WARRANTS

Bonds with warrants give you the right to purchase an additional bond or note at an initially attractive fixed price for a specified period of time. Warrants are sometimes offered to quiet your apprehension concerning the dangers of investing in fixed-income bonds. They are offered more often, however, to entice you to invest in supposedly high-risk municipals. (New York's Municipal Assistance Corporation provided an example of this.) When you invest in municipal bonds with warrants, you must consider whether or not the circumstances of the issuing authority will improve. If they do, and interest rates fall, your warrants will improve in value. If they do not, you may find that your warrants are not worth exercising. Remember that the offer of a warrant shows that investors are reluctant to accept the issuer's straight bond sales offers—maybe with good reason. This is true of any "hybrid" security, including convertible stock.

ZERO-COUPON BONDS ARE WEALTH BUILDERS

Zero-coupon bonds return no periodic payment of interest. Rather, these bonds are offered at a deep discount, and you take your profit when you cash them in at maturity. In other words, your profit is the difference between the price you paid for the bond and the amount of money you receive when you redeem the bond. In fact, you can receive twenty or thirty times your original investment at maturity. A simple example of a zero-coupon bond is the Series E government savings bond, which yields its entire return on maturity. A municipal tax-exempt zero-coupon bond is a security whose interest is reinvested until the bond reaches maturity—in short, the interest is compounded. Of course, zero-coupon bonds increase in value as interest is accumulated and they approach the maturity date. You would find it easy to hold zero-coupon bonds, for you do not have to clip bond coupons, mail them back to the municipal issuer, or keep a record of all your coupons. Furthermore, as with other fixed income investments, the interest rate on a new zero-coupon bond does not fluctuate even if the market rate declines before the bonds come due. Because you receive your return on the bond only when it matures, you do not have to worry about reinvesting any dividends or the proceeds of called bonds quickly at a possibly lower rate of interest. However, this is true only if you buy on the original offering. Zero's purchased in the secondary market can experience a drastic reduction in yield if called before the maturity date. This effect is exaggerated if a premium was paid when making the purchase in the secondary market.

Since 1981 there has been a proliferation of new types of municipal securities known as zero-coupon bonds, compound-coupon bonds, compound-interest bonds or simply "multipliers." The average maturity tends to be eighteen years or longer, and the potential yield on such zero-coupon bonds can be substantially greater than on current coupon bonds.

Both professional and individual investors should be quite cautious about investing blindly in zero-coupon bonds—more cautious than they would have to be about investing in ordinary current coupon bonds or ordinary discount bonds—because zero-coupon bonds have a number of distinct risks as well as some distinct advantages. George D. Friedlander in a research report for Smith Barney Harris Upham and Company summarized the advantages and disadvantages of zero-coupon bonds and "multipliers."

The basic advantages of zero-coupon bonds are these:

1. The yield to maturity, or at least to the first call date, is "locked in," and so there is no reinvestment risk.
2. They are relatively inexpensive and thus are attractive to the small investor.
3. For the investor who expects yields to decline, zero-coupon bonds represent a good opportunity for capital gains, since their value rises much faster, for a 2 percent fall in interest rates, than current coupon bonds do.

However these benefits must be weighed against a large number of negative considerations. The disadvantages include:

1. The market for zero-coupon bonds is quite volatile. For a given change in interest rates, the market value of a twenty-year zero yielding 10 percent will move roughly two and a half times as fast as the market value of a twenty-year 10 percent current coupon bond.
2. In fixed-income securities, greater market volatility is normally correlated with higher yield. This is the most important reason for the positive slope of the municipal yield curve on current coupon bonds. Investors in such bonds require higher returns on bonds that possess

greater potential volatility. In an "efficient" market, one would expect this concept to apply to zeros as well. That is, the yield on the more volatile zeros would exceed that of current coupon bonds of similar maturity.

3. While zeros offer a stable nominal yield, current coupon bonds will probably offer a more stable real rate of return.

4. The implications of a future default are far more severe for purchasers of zero-coupon bonds than for purchasers of current coupon bonds. Holders of current coupon 10 percent, twenty-year bonds will already have received 61.4 percent of their investment back after ten years, on a present value basis, if a default occurs at that time. Holders of zero-coupon bonds will have received nothing and could experience substantial losses, even if the default is subsequently cleared up. Consequently, purchasers of zero-coupon bonds should be especially concerned about the credit ratings of the bonds they buy.

5. If the credit rating of the issuer declines, the market value of a zero will fall much more sharply than that of a current coupon bond of the same maturity. For example, we estimated that for a hypothetical issuer, a downgrading from A to Baa would result in an 8 percent loss of market value for a twenty-year current bond. For that same issuer, a twenty-year zero would lose roughly 25 percent of its market value as a result of the downgrading!

6. Purchasers of an out-of-state zero who live in a state that taxes out-of-state bonds will owe

state income tax on the imputed interest on the zero, even though they do not receive that interest until maturity. The result is a negative cash flow on the zero in each year prior to maturity.

7. Investors who expect yields to drop sharply will have greater appreciation potential on deep-discount bonds that originally sold at par, since these bonds generally offer far greater call protection than zeros do.

Another risk—and to my mind an important one—involves callable zero-coupon bonds. Most of a zero-coupon bond's appreciation takes place in the very last years of its total maturity. If the municipal bond issuer of a zero decides to call that bond prior to that dramatic rise in value in the very last years, the investors have not only locked their money up in a non-income-producing bond for this entire period but have also lost the high expected return, most of which will not even remotely be realized. Because of this danger of calls, some firms, such as E. F. Hutton, have offered better than average call premiums on all callable zeros, thereby paying more than the zeros' very slow accumulated value. However, even this is not a guarantee that investors will receive anywhere near their original expected return.

There are now non-callable zero-coupon bonds and insured zero-coupon bonds available which offer you a great deal of protection and great growth potential.

One good way to finance your retirement years, or to pay for your children's college years is to buy $2,000 worth of zero coupon bonds each year for the next ten years. These ten $2,000 worth of zeros will each mature separately in 15 or 20 years paying you $40,000 each year for 10 years from the day you retire, or the day your first child enters college. Buying zeros in these strips of years is cheap for you to finance each year and is a good way to plan long term and to build wealth.

10

SWAPPING BONDS

Investors often sell municipal bonds before they mature and buy others.

This is called a bond swap. Bond swaps can give you flexibility and strategic control over many objectives at the same time—earnings, safety, and inflation protection.

There are many reasons to swap bonds:

- To minimize taxes
- To consolidate odd lots of bonds
- To raise credit quality
- To adjust maturity
- To diversify geographically
- To increase yield
- To diversify into different types of bonds
- To achieve capital gains
- To achieve triple tax exemption
- To make very short-term arbitrage profits

To *minimize taxes*, you might sell bonds at a loss and buy other bonds with the same maturity, coupon, and credit quality to offset capital gains and other taxes. Of course, you also might sell your bonds at a profit to offset other losses. To indicate how you can gain a number of advantages from a swap, consider the following example.

CLASSIC EXAMPLES

Suppose that you had some older housing bonds that you now could sell only at a discount price of $800 per $1,000 bond. Would it be worth it to you to sell your bonds, take the tax loss, and purchase another bond in a swap?

Yes! It might be well worth it. You could report that tax loss of $200 per bond on your IRS return and simultaneously purchase different discount-priced housing bonds selling at $800 per $1,000 bond but that were substantially identical in all major characteristics to the housing bonds you sold: in credit quality, coupon, yield, and principal amount. In other words, you sell one set of discounted housing bonds, take the tax loss, and buy another, nearly identical set of discounted housing bonds, but from a different-name housing bond issuer. This is the classic tax swap.

Your discount price of $800 per $1,000 bond means that you can declare a loss of $200 per bond you own. If you own ten bonds you can deduct $200 loss per bond or $2,000 on your tax return this year. If you own one hundred bonds then you multiply your $200 loss per bond by one hundred bonds and take a $20,000 loss on your tax return.

THE CLASSIC SINGLE BOND SWAP

Discount price	Face value Par value	Credit rating	Coupon	Maturity	Yield
Sell $80,000	$100,000	Aa housing bond in upper Manhattan	7½%	5/1/95	9.00%
Buy $80,000	$100,000	Aa housing bond in lower Manhattan	7½%	5/1/95	9.00%

THE CLASSIC MULTIPLE BOND TAX SWAP

Discount price	Face value Par value	Credit rating	Coupon	Maturity	Yield
Sell $40,000	$50,000	Aa Los Angeles housing bond	7%	5/1/98	9.00%
$40,000	$50,000	Aa Los Angeles power bond	7%	5/1/98	10.00%
Average Coupon	7%				
Average Life	13 years				
Average Yield	9.5%				
Buy $40,000	$50,000	Aa San Francisco housing bond	8%	5/1/98	8.75%
$40,000	$50,000	Aa San Francisco power bond	6%	5/1/98	10.25%
Average Coupon	7%				
Average Life	13 years				
Average Yield	9.5%				

What did you accomplish by this bond swap? Two things: (1) you established a loss for tax purposes; and (2) you now own essentially the same bonds at a new lower cost.

In fact, after a thirty-one-day waiting period you can even buy back the bonds that you owned originally, if you are willing to take the chance that interest rates won't change drastically during that period.

In the classic multiple example you are swapping bonds of exactly the same type and quality. Although the bonds have a different price and coupons, they have the same *average yield*. In the swap you booked a $20,000 loss for tax purposes, while retaining the same investment features.

ANOTHER EXAMPLE

Suppose that your company transfers you from Massachusetts to California and you wish to keep the multiple tax exemption of your current municipal bond portfolio. Suppose also that you seek, in the required swap, to maintain or increase credit quality but that you do not want to extend the maturity of the new California bonds you are going to buy more than five years beyond the maturity of your Massachusetts bonds. Assume that you refuse to add any new principal and that you wish to maintain your current par value, coupon, and income level.

You would sell your Massachusetts general-obligation bonds:

- Rated by Moody's: A
- Rated by Standard & Poor's: A+

- Coupon: 8.20 %
- Maturity: 2013, uncallable
- Par value: $50,000

Let us assume that you bought fifty bonds originally at $1,000 each and that over the years, and because of rising interest rates, your bonds are now worth only $800 each. Your estimated loss is $200 per bond for a total tax loss of $10,000 on your original investment of $50,000. This means that you wish to take this tax loss of $10,000 to offset your capital gains for the year and to invest the remaining $40,000 from the sale proceeds in new higher-yield bonds of the same type, safety, coupon, and similar maturity.

Having moved to California, you might buy California general-obligation bonds:

- Rated by Moody's: A1
- Rated by Standard & Poor's: AA
- Coupon: 8.25 %
- Maturity: 2015, uncallable
- Par value: $50,000

Let us assume that you must pay a current market price on these new bonds of $740 per bond, or $37,000. Now, let us summarize exactly what you have achieved and how this swap met your original objectives.

Your Goals in Making This Bond Swap	What You Accomplished by This Bond Swap
You sought to achieve a tax loss.	You achieved a tax loss valued at $10,000.

Your Goals in Making This Bond Swap	*What You Accomplished by This Bond Swap*
You sought to increase your current annual income.	You slightly increased your annual income but only by $25 a year.
You sought to upgrade your credit quality for both Moody's and Standard & Poor's ratings.	You succeeded in upgrading your credit quality. Your Moody's rating rose from A to A1 and the Standard & Poor's rating rose from A+ to AA.
You sought *not* to add any new principal.	In fact, you were able to take out $3,000 in principal, and you did not have to put up any new money.
You wished to maintain your par value.	You succeeded in maintaining your par value at $50,000.
You sought to retain triple tax exemption on your bonds.	You succeeded in swapping from triple-tax-exempt Massachusetts bonds to double-tax-exempt California bonds.
You sought not to extend maturity more than five years.	You extended maturity on the bond swap by only two years.

FIVE OTHER KEY STRATEGIES
FOR BOND SWAPS

To consolidate odd lots of bonds, you might sell holdings of several different bonds of five each, adding up to twenty-five bonds. You would suffer a loss when you sell these odd lots because dealers don't like to handle them and will pay you less for them than for a round lot. But you can gain in the long run if you are subsequently forced to sell before maturity because the round lot of twenty-five will command a greater price than five odd lots sold at distress.

To raise credit quality, you might sell bond holdings with a low rating and buy bonds with a higher rating. You do this to lower the risk of default or to avoid a decrease in the value of the bonds if interest rates begin to rise. Perhaps the most common reason for upgrading a municipal bond portfolio, however, would be brought about in situations when spreads between the yields of high-grade bonds and low-grade bonds have narrowed. In this case it is no longer worthwhile to buy a Baa or lower-rated bond when all you might gain would be an extra 40 basis points over what you could earn on an AAA bond. This is called the "flight to quality."

Often such flights to quality are associated with, or immediately accompany, a general perception of rising interest rates and increasingly tight money. In such instances there is sometimes a question as to whether issuers of unrated or lower-rated bonds will be able to pay back the full principal and interest of their obligations.

Such flights to quality can also take place when money is very plentiful and there is a glut of securities of one type or another on the market at one time. Housing bonds at the end of 1980 or public power bonds in 1982 are two examples of this phenomenon. These flights to quality may also involve the risk of having to sell bonds with a low rating at a loss—especially if interest rates are rising and the spreads are widening.

To adjust the maturity of your bonds, you could sell those that are not scheduled to come due for many years. If you decided to swap long-term for short-term bonds, you might possibly take advantage of new bonds being issued with current higher interest rates or you might increase your liquidity. With shorter-term bonds, you would be able to move comparatively quickly out of bonds and into other investments or even speculations like gold. Conversely you might want to consider a move from short-term bonds into longer-term issues if interest rates appear to be decreasing in the future—that is, you might want to lock up your money at a prevailing high yield.

Diversification might be advisable if you hold bonds that are threatened by default or a drastic loss in value. A few years ago, to achieve geographic diversity, many investors got rid of their New York City securities in favor of those issued by Sunbelt states. Likewise, after the Three Mile Island incident, difficulties with other nuclear power plants, and local opposition to new plants, many bondholders decided to diversify and to sell some of their holdings in nuclear power bonds. It is a good idea to avoid heavy investment in issues that could suffer in value from economic, legal, political, or social crises that could arise.

To increase yield, you may decide to switch to bonds that are selling at a deep discount. This would be appropriate when interest rates appear to be declining. These bonds usually appreciate in value much faster than do par bonds, premium bonds, or recent issues. On the Street this is known as the "run to the coupon."

EXAMPLE: SWITCHING TO BONDS SELLING AT A DISCOUNT

Suppose you expect interest rates to drop over the next year or two and you want to swap your high-coupon bond for a lower-coupon bond that will rise in price. You spot a thirty-year bond with a 6 percent coupon that is priced at $51.50 for $100.00 of par value—that is, you would pay $51,500 for a bond that at maturity would be redeemed for $100,000. If you buy at this discount price, your effective yield for the 6 percent coupon would really be 12 percent on your investment.

If during the next six months yields drop 2 percent or 200 basis points, the discount bond you bought at $51.50 per $100 would rise in price to $61.50. As the following simple calculation shows, you'd book a 20.6 percent increase in the value of the discounted bond.

$$\frac{51.50}{61.50} = 20.6\%$$

However, all of the 20.6 percent increase in value of the discounted bonds is not tax exempt. If you sell the bonds and take the profit, you will have to pay capital gains. Consult your accountant about such tax questions. Capital gains do not apply to the increase in value of the appreciation of bonds that are original discount issues or to zero-coupon bonds.

In addition to the potential capital gains from swapping into discount bonds in a period of declining yields, there are other advantages. Such swaps possess substantially lower risk of being called, and they offer a lower reinvestment risk that could prevent you from reinvesting your interest income at the same yield you could with premium or par bonds.

You should understand, however, that par or premium coupon bonds usually provide a more reliable and often higher return than other bonds. Nevertheless, you might consider swapping high-quality for low-quality bonds, in terms of credit ratings, if the yield turns out to be significantly greater.

You also might increase your income by buying triple-tax-exempt bonds—especially if you move to another state. Finally, in times of inflation you could switch from older bonds to new issues, which are likely to sell at better rates than older bonds under these circumstances.

To take short-term arbitrage profits, investors who follow the market conditions closely seek out temporarily undervalued bonds. They sell currently overpriced securities in the same transaction. These swaps require a definite sophistication and a wide knowledge of the market; they are made to secure a better yield.

PROBLEMS ENCOUNTERED
IN MAKING TAX SWAPS

As an individual investor who holds only a few bonds, you may have trouble swapping, because dealers are not very accommodating when only a few bonds are involved in a transaction. You will confront another problem if you are contemplating a swap: the expenses involved in selling and buying bonds. You will have to pay commissions to your broker, settlement expenses, and custodial fees. Then you may owe taxes on many items: capital gains, income, withholding, transfer, and turnover. In fact, your possible gain on a swap could be wiped out completely by these expenses and taxes. Calculate these costs carefully before you decide to swap. You also must take into account a cost that is not so obvious—the spread between the bid and the asked price. That is, you must determine if the profit will be great enough to warrant the transaction. Before you make a swap, you also should be aware that the sums for the swapped bonds rarely will match. You either will have to pay money in order to swap or find some place to invest the money that you are paid back.

Finally, there is the "wash sale rule" to contend with.

This prohibits you from taking a tax credit if you swap bonds for other identical bonds. The Internal Revenue Service will not allow you to take any losses you have incurred from such a sale as an offset against gains, as far as tax credit or deduction is concerned. However, you can make a "no-change swap" by selling two bonds that were sold by the same issuer—one with a maturity ten years longer than the other—in order to purchase one midterm maturity bond from the same issuer. All the other characteristics of the bonds sold and then of those bought remain the same. According to the wash sale rule, the Internal Revenue Service specifies that you may not sell a bond and then buy back substantially the same bond to take a tax loss. In short, the new bond you buy must be somewhat different in at least one key feature, such as coupon, maturity date, or name of issuer.

TIMING YOUR TAX SWAP

In the overwhelming majority of cases you should not wait until the very end of the year to take your tax losses. You should be on the lookout for the exact moment when a swap or loss will be most opportune for you. Selling at the end of the year could be disadvantageous for you because the market is often in a terrible condition at that time, and there are few substantial bargains or few very good bonds to swap into. The market may be busy, frantically trying to deal with a large number of investors and institutions who desperately want to make their own last-minute swaps. If that happens, your swap may not be completed in time to be recorded for the year's tax deduction.

To the contrary, if you are looking for a profit, you should be willing to swap your bonds at any time. For example, in January 1982 the very highest municipal bond yields on record were available. This was a most advantageous time to swap into higher-yield municipal bonds. Obviously, no investors contemplating swaps in January could have predicted with certainty exactly what would happen to interest rates up to the year's end. Interest rates could have soared even higher during the next eleven months. However, the chances were at least even that the national interest rates would come down by the end of the year. Also, coupon rates were at their all-time high and hence were likely to decline. In this instance, the beginning of the year rather than the end of the year was the best time to swap bonds for the purpose of gaining profits.

ADDING CAPITAL
TO ACCOMPLISH A SWAP

The ideal swap involves no loss of principal and requires no new cash. However, such an ideal swap is not always possible. You usually must decide whether to pay in new cash in order to do a bond swap. You must also determine how much new capital you would have to add in order to accomplish a swap. These are not easy questions and there is no single answer to suit all investors. In general, it is never wise to lose principal in order to do a swap to gain profits. However, bond dealers may strongly advise you to make an additional cash investment to accomplish the swap. For instance, if you are holding old low-coupon bonds and you wish to buy new high-coupon bonds, your dealer might well advise you to add extra cash to protect yourself against further price erosions of your old low-coupon bonds. Bond dealers will also argue that you will earn back that additional capital in the higher coupons that you receive on the new bonds. Both of these claims or arguments may, at times, be true. However, you must ask yourself whether these bond salesmen are correct or whether they are simply pressing you hard to buy more bonds and add to your investment in order to enhance their commissions. Basically, you must decide for yourself if this is a good time to put more money into the bond market.

11

YIELD-SPREAD ANALYSIS OF MUNICIPAL TAX-FREE SECURITIES

As an investor, you should always consider the yield-spread differential of a bond before you commit yourself. Most of the time the largest incremental gains in the yield (in terms of percentage return) occur during the first fifteen years. In fact, usually more than 70 percent of the maturity yield is earned in the first fifteen years. By contrast, frequently only 5 percent or less is returned for each five years the bond is held after the first fifteen years. In short, you usually will not get that much extra yield for choosing bonds with long maturities. The best source of this information is the Delphis Hanover range of curve scales, described earlier.

You should always look at exactly where the yield starts to decrease in value. Is the additional .4 percent, or 40 basis points, in yield you get by keeping a bond for an additional ten or twenty years or longer really to your advantage? Alternatively, is it worth it to tie up your money for that extra twenty years if a full 1.5 or 2 percent, or 200 basis points, in extra yield can be obtained from buying very much longer-term bonds? Always check what percentage of the return is earned in the first five to ten years as opposed to the percentage earned in twenty or thirty years. In other words, at what point are you maximizing your return on this bond—that is, gaining extra yield—in exchange for your willingness to stretch the maturity?

Next, you should ask how much extra yield you would receive from an A-rated bond compared with how much you would receive from an AAA-rated bond. You may see that an A-rated bond will pay you .5 percent, or 50 basis points, more than an AAA-rated bond at one point, and at another time pay you 2 percent or 200 basis points, more for your willingness to invest in a bond with a lower credit rating. Once again, you should look not only at the absolute dollars of extra yield but also at the percent of reward of extra yield over this credit-rating range.

For immediate investment purposes you rarely are seriously interested in more than one or two particular bonds. Take those two bonds and do a performance analysis on them to see what advantage you would gain by buying a longer-term bond, or by accepting bonds with a lower credit rating.

Compare these yield spreads for your bond to those in the Bond Buyer Index published each week in *The Bond Buyer*. This will tell you how the average bond is rewarding investors in longer-term bonds or in bonds with lower credit ratings.

Investors should note that the yields to be gained from bonds with the same maturity differ greatly depending on whether the bonds are high-grade, medium-grade, or low-grade. For instance, low-grade bonds will sell at levels closer to the yields of high-grade bonds during periods of rising interest rates than they will during falling markets.

When the spread relationship is very narrow, it probably makes more sense to buy the higher-grade bonds for the relatively small extra yield attainable. By the same token, when the yield gap is very wide in a single maturity between the various credit grades of bonds, the extra credit analysis required to take advantage of the much greater yields offered by the lower-grade bonds is well worth the effort. Additionally, if your own investment policy permits it, you will see that it has always made sense to sell lower-grade bonds when the spread between them and higher-grade bonds has contracted and to reinvest in the higher-grade bonds, and vice versa. In this way you can take advantage of the spread differentials in your favor.

FALLING BOND MARKETS

As we have said, the bond market falls as interest rates rise. Rising interest rates are a product of some combination of inflationary pressure, heightened demand for available capital, Federal Reserve policy, and investors' lack of confidence in the stability of the bond market. Another factor can cause a falling market for municipal bonds—the potential threat that Congress will eliminate or alter their tax-exempt status.

RISING BOND MARKETS

The bond market rises as interest rates fall. Falling interest rates are the product of some combination of the following: recessionary pressure, lessened demand for available capital, Federal Reserve policy, and confidence by investors that the bond market will strengthen or will not continue to erode.

Investment Strategies in a Rising Market: When Yields Fall

1. Buy long-term discount bonds if possible. They will outperform all other bonds in a rising market.
2. Premium bonds will hurt the value of your portfolio in a rising market. The larger the premium the smaller the market for the bonds, because few institutional buyers of bonds are willing to buy the higher and higher premium bonds. That is, your buyer base narrows quite sharply as you try to sell higher and higher premium bonds.
3. Watch the call provisions. Be very careful to avoid an early call.

Investment Strategies in a Falling Market: When Yields Rise

1. In a falling bond market—when interest rates are rising—you should buy securities with shorter and shorter maturities, because you don't need to reach for yield, nor do you need to buy long-term bonds in order to achieve a comfortable non-callable yield.
2. In a falling market you can either refuse to buy callable bonds or search for bonds with a much later call provision. You don't want the issuers to take these bonds away from you after you have chosen a long maturity specifically to lock

into a very high yield. Let them call the bonds indirectly by pre-refunding them. Pre-refunding results when a municipal bond–issuing authority in effect pays off the bond issue early by purchasing guaranteed U.S. government bonds to replace the municipal bond issue so that the municipality can start issuing new municipal bonds at the currently far more favorable—i.e., lower—rate.

3. Swap yourself all the way down the falling market to take advantage of the ever higher yields. This is one of the most successful strategies for investing in a falling market.

THE INDIVIDUAL INVESTOR'S STRATEGY: A WARNING

As an individual investor in municipal bonds, you should always remember that when you invest in *any* long-term bonds you are gambling with interest rates. You are not in the same position as institutional investors or very wealthy individuals who can afford to hold bonds through a period of declining interest rates and who can take tax losses involved in swapping out of bonds that are performing poorly. If you are an average individual investor, you cannot absorb substantial losses. Therefore, you would be wise to buy only tax-exempt municipal bonds or notes that will mature in one or two years—or whatever length of time you know you can hold the bonds. If you do this, you will not have to sell your bonds before they mature.

Remember that a municipal bond will pay principal *at maturity*. So from the day you purchase the bond until the day it matures, the value of your principal is subject to the vagaries of the inflation rate, interest-rate changes, government fiscal policy changes, and Federal Reserve monetary policy changes. And these possible fluctuations are in addition to the adverse effects of a severe recession on the bond issuer, or a municipal bond default, or financial crisis of some other sort.

Remember, too, that the less you know about municipal bonds, the greater chance you have of getting burned. If you lock yourself into high-yield but *very* long-term municipal bonds, for example, you might have to sell them at a loss prior to maturity if interest rates rise or because of some unforeseen personal circumstance. Thus, it is wise to buy short-term bonds or put bonds. That way, you will at least keep up with inflation.

CHAPTER

12

CREDIT ANALYSIS OF GENERAL-OBLIGATION BONDS

The funds from general-obligation bonds are used to finance the running of cities and states, the building of public schools and firehouses, the purchase of police cars, and the maintenance of city streets, libraries, hospitals, and many other municipal services. They are vital to city governments, and yet, before 1975 little analysis of the security of general-obligation municipal bonds was made by bank trust departments, insurance company portfolio managers, or Wall Street firms. Because communities had the legal right to levy a variety of taxes, many people assumed that their bonds would be among the safest and least volatile of investments. Bondholders also thought that they would be the first to be paid if the municipality faced the supposedly remote prospect of default.

The New York City financial crisis of 1975 quickly changed that thinking. Investors suddenly realized that default can occur even in apparently solid communities when a municipal government is so short of funds that it can do only one of two things: (1) it can pay off its bondholders, *or* (2) it can pay the salaries of its police officers, fire fighters, health-care workers, and other indispensable city employees. The credit analysis that is now carried out on general-obligation bonds largely results from this realization.

A credit analysis of bonds is based on several different considerations: (1) the debt burden, (2) budget and audits, (3) administration, (4) revenues of the state or city that is issuing bonds, and (5) the economic health of the issuer. Thus, Moody's municipal credit rating department compares a municipality's debt to its assessments on housing and individual and commerical property, tax collections, income level, and budget—in short, the ratio of debt to wealth. Standard & Poor's looks closely at each municipality's per capita growth trends and personal income growth or decline. Also, Standard & Poor's studies a community's property assessments and the type of property—whether commercial, industrial, or residential. Each rating agency tries to obtain the same background information, but each one weighs the elements differently to determine the credit rating.

Moody's Standard & Poor's, and Fitch (the third national rating agency) indicate creditworthiness with symbols that are relatively similar. But, in addition to using the so-called "standard rating categories" of Aaa for the highest rate to C for the lowest, Moody adds a superscript 1 in categories A through Baa which they estimate possess the strongest investment attributes; Standard & Poor's and Fitch use + and − in categories AA to BB to indicate either added strengths or weaknesses.

Usually, the credit rating of a municipality will be quite similar for all three rating agencies. Quite different ratings or "split ratings" occur daily but are less common. The following example shows how each of the rating services might assign a very *different* rating to the same municipality.

Standard & Poor's gave an AA rating to general-obligation bonds of Allegheny County, Pennsylvania, after observing a steady growth of the economy in the region and an increase in the wealth of the population. The analysis showed that industry had diversified and that the area was now less dependent on the steel industry. Standard & Poor's also saw that budgetary and accounting procedures were being improved and debt was being retired rapidly.

Moody's, however, gave the bonds a Baa1 rating because Allegheny County had a high debt load and was considering the sale of even more bonds for highway and bridge repairs and for the construction of a new hospital. The county also had unfunded pension liabilities. Moody's also concluded (1) that Allegheny County used unorthodox accounting procedures that shifted taxation from the county to the districts and (2) that it assessed property values according to archaic criteria.

The rating services clearly warn that a rating is not a recommendation to purchase, sell, or hold a security. Nor do the agencies comment on the market price or suitability of a bond issue for any particular investor. The symbols AAA through C do not mean that the rating service has performed an audit on the issuing authority or determined the veracity of the information it has received. The rating agencies simply assess the likelihood of default and try to determine whether a bond issue is *investment grade* or *speculative grade*. As mentioned earlier, bonds with the four highest ratings—AAA, AA, A, and BBB— are regarded as investment grade, whereas bonds rated below BBB are considered speculative. Many investors and institutions avoid these lower-rated bonds, and trust departments and other professional institutional investors are legally prohibited from investing in them.

Moody's considers *debt* the most important criterion in establishing a credit rating. It studies the municipality's debt trend for at least the past five years to see if the city has sunk increasingly deeper in debt and if so, it also finds out if repayment of this debt is guaranteed—either by a draw on a cash fund balance or from tax revenue.

Most general-obligation bonds are secured by the taxing powers of the government issuing the bonds. Some, however, are *also* supported by specific revenue sources such as tolls or rent income. These are called *double-barreled bonds* and should be considered more secure than "straight" general-obligation bonds that are backed only by a pledge of the taxing power. The *net obligation debt*, then, is the amount of bonds outstanding that are backed by tax income from the general fund only. In addition the analyst must find out how much debt from other bond-issuing authorities must be retired with income from the tax base of the government that is now offering bonds. If the issuer is a city, it might have diverted some of its potential tax-based income to service county or school district bonds. This is called *overlapping debt*. In reverse, a county government might be responsible for some debt incurred by, or in behalf of, a municipality; this must be considered if the county government or agency issues bonds. This is called *underlying debt*. (The general obligation of debt of state governments usually is not considered when municipal or county bonds are being rated because state governments have revenue sources other than the property taxes that constitute the major income of most local governments.)

Issuers that are committed to policies that require them to borrow large amounts of money are clearly less attractive than those that have coordinated their indebtedness to rely on small amounts of short-term debt. However, the analyst must also consider the percentage that short-term debt takes from the general fund because short-term debt must be constantly reissued, or rolled over, each year.

All other sizable debt obligations of that municipality must be considered when the credit rating of bonds is made. Many state and local governments have entered into leasing agreements for new buildings, office space, and computers, among other things. These obligations must be paid from general funds derived from the same sources of taxes and fees from which bonds and notes must be serviced. In addition, many states issue bonds backed by a debt service reserve fund that is usually funded when the bonds are first sold and replenished from taxes or revenues. Most of these bonds are supported by taxes or fees and the pledge is not drawn from, but some have required the states to draw from the fund. Two bonds of this sort are issued by the Pennsylvania Housing Finance Agency and the South Jersey Port

Corporation. The states then must restore the money withdrawn. This potential liability should be considered when the state bonds are being evaluated. Unfunded pension liabilities also must be noted. The liability is the difference between the income that can be anticipated from pension fund contributors and the outgo to be paid to retired and retiring employees. To arrive at what is called a *special debt figure*, lease obligations, moral obligations, and pension liabilities are combined, and the total amount is one element in evaluating a bond issue.

Finally, the rating agencies and all credit analysts must assess the potential impact of tax limitations. These restrictions may be beneficial or harmful to general-obligation bondholders. For example, such tax limitations have forced many municipalities to improve their budgets, revise their accounts, and increase their financial control. However, such tax limits (sometimes called caps laws) could adversely affect holders of overlapping bonds. In addition, certain general-obligation bonds issued by states can be adversely affected if municipalities, restricted by caps laws, are forced to turn to the state government for funds if those funds have to be drawn from the state surplus.

Aside from evaluating debt arising from general obligations and the special debt, the analyst must establish the municipality's *straight-revenue debt*. This obligation is backed by tolls and fees, and the agencies issuing bonds have *no legal claim* on the general tax income of a state or municipality. However, if a city toll bridge authority were to default or go bankrupt, then the city and/or state might feel obligated to step in and help bail out that toll bridge authority simply in order to protect that city's or state's ability to meet its *own* debt needs in the bond market. Otherwise, that city or state might be tainted by the toll bridge authority's default, and the bond market might punish the city by demanding an exorbitant cost when it next tries to issue bonds. Though this straight-revenue bond is not factored into debt ratios of the city or state in which the agency is located, you should be aware of the ability of the agency to handle its debt and the impact any financial crisis might have on the particular municipality or state.

The analyst must learn the future financing plans of the authority that is issuing bonds. Although one municipality already has large amounts of bonds to finance, an analyst nevertheless might rate that municipality's new issue higher than new bonds from a second municipality that currently has only a small amount of debt outstanding but faces the prospect of going heavily into debt in the future.

The *form of government* of the bond issuer will also affect the rating a bond issue might be given. "Strong" mayors, governors, or centralized executive systems with authority over budget preparation, veto rights over the budget, control over its implementation, and the power to hire or fire can deal quickly and efficiently with unexpected budgetary and economic problems. "Weak" governments are restricted by the requirement that electoral approval must be given before action can be taken. Many also believe that a chief executive elected for only a short term may concentrate on reelection rather than a sound financing policy. Thus, Detroit had very serious economic problems but avoided default because the government was strong. Cleveland, with a weaker form of government and a less serious economic problem than Detroit, did default. Bonds issued by strong governments are naturally preferred to those offered by weaker governments.

In order to project budgetary demands, the analyst must also know what services the issuer provides. Issuers that provide only the minimum—water, sewage, and police and fire protection—usually receive a higher rating than municipalities that provide a much wider variety of services—welfare, hospital care, and higher education—whose recipients may demand the services regardless of budgetary considerations.

Accounting procedures must also be evaluated. The most acceptable procedure is the modified accrual system by which revenues are considered to have been received only when they are actually in the general fund. Analysts must look out for governments that use less stringent practices. For example, to balance their budgets conveniently, some governments or agencies might define revenue as income that has not actually been received. Or they might create the appearance of a budget surplus by delaying payments due until the next fiscal year has begun. The true state of affairs must be uncovered before an accurate evaluation can be given.

Before a rating is assigned, audit procedures must be clarified. It is most desirable that the issuer be audited annually by an outside certified public accountant. Otherwise, the governmental agency should be audited by an elected official who is politically independent of the chief executive, or by someone appointed by the legislative branch. Other means for obtaining the audit would affect the bond rating to varying degrees—probably negatively.

Along with making an evaluation of debt burden, budget and audit practices, and administrative strength, the bond analyst must review the issuer's *sources of revenue*. The analyst must determine the issuer's (1) primary sources of income (from income taxes, users' fees, and business taxes) and (2) levels of income for the preceding four years. If issuers pay their debt from a debt service fund maintained by taxes that are not passed through the general fund, this fund also is included in the evaluation.

Most analysts require information on the overall economic health of the issuing authority, which should include trends in real estate evaluations, population, rate of unemployment, and total personal income. They want to know the true market values of real estate as opposed to the assessed value. Thus, annual appreciation must outpace increases in inflation. They want to find out how much property is tax abated or tax exempt, and how much new real estate will be exempted. They break down the raw population figures by age group and income level. A community with a high proportion of senior citizens, for instance, may demand more expensive services and reduced property taxes. They have to know the major employers, the nature of the businesses, the number of people employed in comparison with the population overall, the extent to which new people arrive in search of work, and the unemployment trends. Of course, the average income level must be determined as well.

After the analysts have considered all of the variables discussed above, they can attempt to determine the degree of risk a buyer incurs in purchasing the issuer's general-obligation bonds. Even after the analysts have evaluated the mass of accumulated information, they must realize that the process of rating bond issues remains more an art than a science.

CREDIT ANALYSIS OF REVENUE BONDS

The default and potential bankruptcy of the Washington Public Power Supply System bonds, or Woops bonds, in 1983 spurred investors to do more credit analysis of revenue bonds before they invest. Not only was Woops the largest issuer of municipal revenue bonds in the entire nation, but the rating agencies had for years given the Woops bonds strong ratings. Woops bonds were the most widely held bonds by investors of all types. How could this gigantic default and financial crisis have occurred? It happened, quite simply, because almost no one was doing good credit analysis of those famous revenue bonds. Almost every investor—individual, professional, and institutional—simply bought the Woops bonds on blind faith.

This chapter is meant to help you protect yourself against investing in a future municipal revenue bond default or bankruptcy.

Revenue bonds are issued by public agencies to finance projects that are supported by tolls or users' fees. Some of these projects are sewers, gas lines, parking lots, airports, and seaports, which often serve several communities or states. Years ago, bonds were issued to finance canals, turnpikes, and utilities. The return from all these different types of revenue bonds is tax exempt because they serve the public interest.

Some of these bonds are financed under an arrangement by which an authority constructs a facility and then leases it to a municipality or an industry at a rent calculated to pay the interest and principal on the bonds. Some bonds—for urban redevelopment, housing, transit, or pollution control, for instance—are secured by federal government authority. Certain so-called moral-obligation bonds are also backed by a state's pledge to support a debt reserve fund may be used to reimburse the bond issue.

CREDIT ANALYSIS USING FINANCIAL RATIOS

Analysts use a number of financial ratios to test the creditworthiness of revenue bonds:

$$\text{Operating ratio} = \frac{\text{Operating and maintenance expenses}}{\text{Operating revenues}}$$

$$\text{Interest coverage} = \frac{\text{Net revenues}}{\text{Interest payments required}}$$

$$\text{Debt service charge} = \frac{\text{Net revenues}}{\text{Debt service required}}$$

$$\frac{\text{Debt service}}{\text{safety margin}} = \frac{\text{Debt service}}{\text{Gross revenues}}$$

$$\text{Debt ratio} = \frac{\text{Net debt}}{\text{Sum of working capital}\atop\text{plus plant}}$$

$$\text{Net takedown} = \frac{\text{Net revenues}}{\text{Gross revenues}}$$

In doing a credit analysis, the analysts will look at the above ratios and more for each municipal bond. They are looking for signs of strength or weakness. What is the trend in these ratios for this municipality or public authority over the last five years? Are the interest coverage, debt service coverage, and debt service safety margin secure or deteriorating? For example, analysts would probably consider a 1.2 percent debt service coverage strong and healthy because it means that the municipality has plenty of revenues to cover its immediate debt service payments. But they would be concerned if the municipality's debt ratio grows too large because that means the municipality will become more likely to default or to enter a financial crisis.

Water and Sewer Bonds

Water and sewer bonds are thought to be among the safest municipal investments because people must have water and sewers. Ratings are highest in areas that are long established and stable, although government-mandated anti-pollution laws and the expenses arising from them have caused some industries to close or move out of the jurisdiction. Lower ratings are often assigned to newly constructed or rapidly expanding communities because some bonds have been defaulted when the anticipated influx of population failed to materialize.

Basically, a credit analysis of water and sewer bonds involves considering the following:

- What exactly is the water or sewer system that will be financed? Is it really needed?
- What geographic area will the water and sewer system serve?
- What is the current and projected population?
- What has the wealth of the population been in the past? What is it currently? What is it projected to be?
- Who are the major users of the system (big companies, a prison, hospitals, schools)? Will they stay or will they close down?
- What is the water and sewer rate or charge per user? How high is this rate compared to the property tax levy?
- What is the indebtedness of the authority currently? How much is it likely to borrow in the future?
- How much flexibility does the authority have to raise rates? What would the effects of rate changes be?
- What caliber of management does the authority have?

Hospital Bonds

Many hospital bonds are backed only by the ability of the institution's management to generate revenue on its own, although some are guaranteed by federal agencies, and others, particularly teaching hospitals, have large private endowments. In rating hospitals, bond analysts consider factors similar to those used to rate water and sewer bonds, but there are variations. In addition to the basic checklist for revenue bond analysis listed for water and sewer bonds, the hospital bond analyst asks these questions:

- What are the hospital's revenues and expenses?
- How much is this hospital likely to borrow in the future?
- What is the caliber of the hospital's management? How good are the doctors and professional staff?
- What is the socioeconomic class of the hospital's patients?
- How dependent is the hospital on Medicare and Medicaid patients?

Hospital bonds are considered somewhat risky—about 85 percent are rated only A—because they cannot raise income from taxes but only from fees based on the extent to which they are utilized. Hospitals usually must face competition from other hospitals, unlike a water system. Also, there is only a small number of bidders for any one hospital's bonds. So insured hospital bonds have become popular, to increase security and market ability.

Public Power Bonds
Public power bonds constitute the largest share of long-term revenue bonds offered on the market—an

impressive 13 percent. But because of the "Whoops" default many questions must be asked if new issues are to be evaluated accurately. These questions include:

- What legal contractual protection is provided the bondholder, especially by new municipal power authorities?
- Does the authority have sole right to serve a geographic area?
- Are the potential customers willing and able to pay for service?
- Will the utility be able to deliver power at the contracted price?
- Are fuel sources and sources of power available by long-term or short-term contract?
- What are the financial operating statistics?
- What is the projected debt over the next decade?
- How competent and experienced is the management of the power authority?

Analysts must consider the uncertainties involved in completing a new utility. These uncertainties arise from the possibility that construction might not be completed, that it may be delayed for years, or that the engineering could result in an improper or inadequately functioning system. Analysts must rely heavily on the engineer's feasibility study and on governmental requirements. Of course, if an established power authority is offering bonds, analysts consider the utility management's past success in forecasting performance accurately, maintaining rates in line with budget requirements, meeting unusually heavy demands for power, and adhering to long-range plans.

Municipalities recently have begun to form joint utility companies. Joint ownership greatly increases the creditworthiness of the bonds because of the recognized names of one or more of the issuers and their security. The arrangement does not provide absolute protection because a weak participant in the venture could default, forcing the other muncipalities or agencies to assume its obligations and creating an increased financial burden on the other participants. Analysts must ask *whose* credit or security is being pledged for a new enterprise. They must know whether or not the participating muncipalties are "jointly or severally" liable for the guarantee of the bonds or only liable to the degree each is a participant in the project.

Housing Bonds

Housing bonds are by far the most complex revenue bonds to evaluate.

For *direct loan program housing bonds,* real estate developers receive a direct mortgage loan from a state housing finance agency, a public agency, or some other authority to build housing for, say, the elderly or for low- to moderate-income families who receive federal rent subsidies. The bonds are usually secured by, and interest and principal paid from, payments on mortgages, for which part or all is paid from federal subsidies. Additional credit is backed by or sometimes provided by the state government's moral obligation pledge of appropriations if and when the debt service reserve fund is depleted. Although some analysts stress that the primary security behind the bonds is the mortgage payments, others insist that the state government's moral pledge is much more important. Those who regard mortgage payments as more important must assess the entire portfolio of mortgages. Those who rely on the government pledge must look at the state's general-obligation bond rating to determine the worth of housing bonds. Basically, however, different ratings are assigned if the housing bonds are federally insured. However, this is not an entirely reliable basis on which to evaluate bonds, because federally insured housing programs are not always totally guaranteed. For example, the federal government pays 99 percent of the principal on the mortgage. This poses a problem for bond analysts and investors: Where does the remaining 1 percent come from? What happens if the housing developer goes bankrupt or fails to complete the housing? It depends.

Direct loan programs that are *not* insured by the federal government are far more difficult to evaluate because the analyst must carefully consider four things: (1) the nature of the federal rent subsidy, (2) the worth of the state government's moral pledge, (3) the underlying security of the real estate and housing units themselves, and (4) the caliber of the management of the state housing agency, or local agency.

In evaluating the mortgage portfolio of direct loan programs, an analyst cannot examine each mortgage unless the portfolio is small. If additional mortgages can be added and if additional bonds can be sold, the credit evaluation will focus on the process used by the agency to market these new securities. The analyst must find out if the procedures are sound and must decide how competent the staff is.

Taking another approach, analysts consider the balance and composition of the portfolio. They look at the geographic diversity (inner city or suburban or rural), the type of project (for families or for the elderly), the subsidy, and state and local economic conditions.

Mortgage purchase bonds are issued to finance low- and moderate-income single and multi-family housing (Chicago plan or single-city housing bond issues also are offered for homes for higher-income families). The proceeds from the sale of these housing revenue bonds are used to buy mortgages from savings and loan institutions. The bond's principal and interest payments come from mortgage payments.

The distinctions between the different types of mortgage purchase have to do primarily with whether they are offered to finance new construction on a new site or to fund established housing developments, and whether there are small, local groups of mortgages or large, highly diversified pools of mortgages. The small, geographically restricted pool of mortgages calls for a more specific analysis, whereas the larger, more highly diversified pool of mortgages requires an actuarial, or statistical, approach.

Four factors provide the analysts with a basis on which to evaluate mortgage purchase bonds: (1) cash flow, (2) assets, (3) legal protection, and (4) management. All of these are interrelated, of course, and the bond analyst or investor should balance one against the others. Suppose, for example, that the housing bond issuer has limited assets and suppose that real estate, local economics, and the demographics of the area where the project is to be built are poor. These negative factors sometimes can be offset if the municipal housing authority has adequate insurance and an ample flow of cash. The housing assets have to be protected and the cash flow has to be at least sufficient to meet expenses, so analysts do not use an either/or form of analysis. Instead, they assess the strengths and weaknesses of the project for which the bonds are being issued.

The Section 8 Subsidy Program

The U.S. Government Housing Act, Section 8, provides rent subsidies for housing. These subsidies are adjusted as inflation, and the tenants' incomes and ability to pay a greater part of the rent fluctuate. These are very comprehensive subsidies that cover all of the operating expenses as well as the debt service of a housing project.

There are many advantages to be gained from relying on Section 8 programs, but the programs do present some problems to those who try to assess the true value of the housing projects they are being used to fund. First, and most important, the Department of Housing and Urban Development (HUD), which administers Section 8, retains the right to withdraw the subsidy of a project under some circumstances. If the housing project is not fully occupied for an extended period of time or if the units do not meet the department's specific standards for "safe and sanitary" housing, HUD can withdraw its subsidies. Because HUD has the authority to do this, investors and bond analysts must examine each new housing project on its own merits.

Second, the great variety in the range of housing projects themselves must be looked into, e.g., multiple family, low income, and retirement units. Also to be determined is the ability of the project's managers, the extent of the financial reserves held for the housing project, insurance and legal protection for the bondholder, the accuracy of the cost estimates for the housing project, the strength of the trust indenture, the site of the housing project, and the number of people who want to live in the housing project. Related to this last question, the availability of alternative housing, now and in the future, must be surveyed. These factors relate to the vacancy rate of units in the housing project and are of major concern because of HUD's right to terminate subsidies if vacancies last longer than one year.

The financial community regards housing projects backed by Section 8 as very safe for investment because of the guarantees that are made. For example, during the life of the bond contract, the total collected rent from each project is kept in a reserve that HUD can use to adjust its subsidy allotments and to meet increased operating expenses should that become necessary. Appendix 2 at the end of this book explains the U.S. Government Housing Act, Section 8-116.

14

SUMMARY

This chapter provides some suggestions for mapping out a successful investment strategy in tax-exempt municipal securities. It is a summary of all the advice spelled out in detail in earlier chapters.

First, we shall review the advantages and rewards as well as the pitfalls and risks of investing in tax-exempt bonds.

REWARDS

There are three good reasons to build a portfolio of municipal bonds, notes, and commercial paper.

These bonds provide the advantages of financial fixed income security: relative safety, marketability, and liquidity. Furthermore, municipal securities are far more flexible and more versatile fixed income securities now than they were in the past. Individual investors can now choose from a veritable smorgasbord of tax-exempt securities: the many new types of tax-exempt bonds, notes, leases, and commercial paper; many new types of tax-exempt bond funds and tax-exempt money market funds; and many different types of tax-exempt unit trusts.

Obviously federal tax exemption is the key advantage of municipal securities. Triple tax exemption from state and local and federal tax is another added inducement. Here are the other key advantages of municipal securities over taxable securities:

- The after-tax return on tax-free bonds is greater than the return from taxable securities.
- The amount of capital you need to invest in tax-free bonds is less than the amount needed to invest in taxable investments to earn the same after-tax return.
- The length of time that you must tie up your capital in order to earn the same amount of money, after tax, is far shorter in a tax-free bond versus a taxable investment.

RISKS

Default Risks
Most municipal bonds are relatively secure, but always remember that they can involve some risk. There is the slight but serious possibility that the issuing government or agency might default—fail to pay the interest or even the principal when the bond matures. This risk of default can be minimized if you concentrate on buying insured bonds or bonds backed by a bank letter of credit, or general-obligation bonds with the highest credit rating, although each of these

yield interest at a lower percentage than do higher-risk bonds. Or you could buy project notes that are guaranteed by the federal government as well as by the municipality or other issuing agent. Or you could buy so-called double-barreled bonds, which are backed by two or more revenue sources such as taxes and users' fees.

Interest Rate Risks

The value of bonds is sensitive to fluctuations in interest rates. When interest rates go up, the price of bonds tends to fall. Nearly fifteen years of high interest rates caused many bond investors to lose billions in the asset value of their old bonds, purchased before interest rates rose. You can decrease risk somewhat by investing in tax-exempt notes, short-term bonds, funds or put bonds, or variable bonds.

Risk of Lowered Credit Rating

Watch your bonds to see if their rating is likely to be lowered. A lower rating could result from deteriorating financial, economic, or demographic conditions in the municipality or from political pressures such as a taxpayers' revolt. A possible downgrading of credit rating and the value of the bonds might be indicated if the various rating agencies give the municipality's bonds variant ratings. A difference in two agencies' ratings on the same municipality is known as a split rating. Watch for any changes in economic conditions in the area whose government or agency has issued the bonds—such as the crisis in the automobile industry in Detroit. If an economic crisis hits an area, check constantly to see if the price of the bonds has started to change in the market.

Legal Risks

Ask your broker to make sure that the bonds you are considering will not be disqualified for tax exemption. Lawyers and bankers have invented many new types of municipal securities that are based on complicated legal foundations and credit support. It has become more difficult to say with certainty if the Internal Revenue Service will approve each and every bond's tax-free status. Also ask your broker to consider the legality of the bond issuer's contracts. The Washington Public Power Supply System's court cases have demonstrated the importance of this.

Accounting Risk

Finally, make sure that the issuer of the bonds you are considering is following generally accepted accounting procedures. If the issuer is not doing this, your bonds might lose their credit rating or, worse, default. You can determine this from the bond document itself or from the underwriter, or just ask your broker. Find out if short-term debt is being accrued substantially as a substitute for long-term obligation. Also find out whether the issuer is increasingly relying on leased equipment and office space. Also, find out if income from taxes or other government sources is diminishing, and learn the extent of unfunded pensions for employees.

HOW TO BUILD YOUR TAX-EXEMPT PORTFOLIO

Before you decide to invest in municipal bonds, you should answer these questions:

- What is your tax bracket now? What do you expect it to be ten years from now?
- What would your after-tax return be if you invested in tax-exempt bonds? Taxable securities?
- What is the current inflation rate? What do you expect it to be ten years from now?
- What maturity date do you prefer in your bonds? Short, medium or long?
- What type of securities do you desire to hold? What type do you wish to avoid?
- What credit risk are you willing to take on your bonds?
- How much liquidity and marketability do you want in your bond portfolio?
- Are you willing to sell or swap your bonds?

Ask your dealer these questions about any bonds you are considering buying:

- What was the cover on this bond—the difference between the winning bid and the second best bid made by the underwriters? In other words, are these bonds priced competitively?
- What was the size of the bond issue offered? How many bonds remained unsold? In other words, is the bond selling well or badly?
- Why are the bonds being offered at a higher or lower yield than similarly rated bonds sold a week or so before?
- What is the tone of the market? Is it going higher or lower?
- What comparable bonds are being sold on the secondary market and at what price?

YIELD SPREAD ANALYSIS
OF TAX-FREE
MUNICIPAL SECURITIES

Always consider the spread differential of a bond before you commit yourself. Most of the time the largest incremental gains in the yield (in terms of percent return) occur during the first fifteen years. In fact, usually more than 70 percent of the maturity yield is earned in the first fifteen years. Frequently only 5 percent or less is returned for each five years the bond is held after the first fifteen years. In short, you usually will find that you are not getting that much extra yield for going long.

Always find out what percentage of the bond's return is earned in the first five to ten years as opposed to the full twenty or thirty years. In other words, at what point are you maximizing your return on this bond as far as gaining extra yield for your willingness to stretch for extra-long maturity is concerned?

Next, evaluate how much extra yield you are receiving for a bond rated A and how much you would receive for an AAA bond. For example an A-rated bond will pay you 40 basis points more than an AAA bond at one point and at another time may pay you 200 basis points more in return for your willingness to invest in the lower-rated bond. Once again you should look not only at the absolute dollars of extra yield but also at the percent reward of extra yield over this credit rating range.

This analysis might at first seem complex, but in fact it is quite easy. Use Delphis Hanover's yield curve scales for this printed weekly in *The Bond Buyer*.

Compare these yield spreads for your bond to the *Bond Buyer* index to see how bonds in general are rewarding investors in longer-term bonds and in lower-rated bonds at this same moment. The *Bond Buyer* index is published each week in *The Bond Buyer*.

Investors should note that the yields to be gained from bonds with the same maturity differ greatly among high-grade, medium-grade, and low-grade bonds. That is, during periods of rising interest rates low-grade bonds will sell at levels closer to the yields of high-grade bonds than during falling markets.

When the spread is very narrow, it probably makes more sense to buy the higher-grade bonds for the relatively small extra yield attainable. But, by the same token, when the yield gap is very wide in a single maturity between the various credit grades of bonds, the extra credit analysis required to take advantage of the much greater yields offered by the lower-grade bonds is well worth the effort.

FALLING BOND MARKETS

The bond market falls as interest rates rise. Rising interest rates are a product of some combination of inflationary pressure, heightened demand for available capital, Federal Reserve policy, and investors' lack of confidence.

RISING BOND MARKETS

The bond market rises as interest rates fall. Falling interest rates are the product of some combination of recession, lessened demand for available capital, Federal Reserve policy, and investors' confidence.

INVESTMENT STRATEGIES IN A RISING BOND MARKET

When yields begin to fall, take these steps:

1. Buy discount bonds if possible. They will out-perform all other bonds in a rising market.
2. Avoid premium bonds. They will decrease the value of your portfolio in a rising market be-cause the larger the premium the less market there will be for the bonds.
3. Watch the call provisions and take care to avoid an early call.

INVESTMENT STRATEGY IN A FALLING MARKET

When yields begin to rise, take these steps:

1. Concentrate your investment strategy in buy-ing bonds with shorter and shorter maturities.
2. Swap all the way down the falling market to take advantage of the higher yields.

A WARNING CONCERNING INTEREST RATE FLUCTUATIONS

Remember that if you invest in *any* long-term bonds, you are gambling with interest rates. You are not in the same position as institutional investors or very wealthy individuals who can afford to hold bonds through a period of declining interest rates and take a great many tax losses by swapping out of bonds that are performing poorly. As an average individual investor, you cannot absorb substantial losses. Restrict your municipal tax-exempt purchases to periods of one or two years or to exactly the length of time you know you can hold the bonds. Or buy long-term bonds that have a "put," or option for you to sell back your bonds to the issuer in one to five years.

Next, decide what is the best time to buy bonds. Timing is affected by several things:

You may want long-term bonds, to lock up high yields. But check your options.

If you want to build your wealth, or finance your retirement, or your child's college years, purchase zero coupon bonds maturing in 15 or 20 years. But choose only insured zeros, or zeros with very strong credit ratings and with good call protection. By investing $2000 each year for 10 years in zeros you can receive $40,000 each year for 10 years when you retire.

TIMING YOUR INVESTMENT

- The economic health of the nation and the region
- The money supply
- Competition from other bond offerings with similar characteristics or from the U.S. government or corporation issues
- Current or anticipated interest and inflation rates
- The prevailing yields from all bonds (When

government and corporate securities go down, municipal bonds often follow; when U.S. government securities go up, municipal bonds often follow.)

Because the bond market is a buyers' and sellers' market, you should wait for a glut of sellers to materialize before you buy bonds. Conversely, you should wait until many buyers are present before you sell your bonds.

But how do you know when there is a glut of bonds for sale? How can you tell when there is a scarcity? And how do you determine when bonds might increase or decrease in value? By indicators.

Be aware of a number of indicators that predict bond performance. Here are some general economic conditions that are *most* favorable to purchasing bonds:

- Declining rates of inflation
- Declining interest rates
- Stable money supply
- Flexible Federal Reserve policy
- Limited federal government demand for money
- Limited corporate demand for money

Above all, however, consider the following specific bond market indicators:

- The first and most important ratio reflects the yield percentage on tax-exempt bonds as compared to taxable bonds. This AAA municipal U.S. government ratio tells you how well you are being rewarded for buying tax-exempt bonds as opposed to taxable bonds. When this ratio is *at least 75 percent*, you should consider investing in municipals.

- The next bond market indicators you should look at are the Delphis Hanover range of yield curve scales and new issue reports because they show the comparison between the bond you are considering and many other current bonds. This tells you which has the better price and rate of return for each year of maturity. This helps you to find bargains and to avoid buying over-priced bonds.
- The third bond market indicator, the *Bond Buyer*'s placement ratio, is useful because it indicates how well new bond issues are selling. If there is suddenly a glut of bonds on the market and new bonds are not selling well, then you may find some bargains because many bonds will have to be priced lower in order to attract buyers.
- The last bond market indicators are the par value of the Blue List of secondary bond offerings and the thirty-day visible supply of new bonds, which together indicate the current supply of bonds on the market and the number of bonds very soon to be issued.

After you have built a portfolio of bonds, keep in mind the changing financial conditions of the country and each of your bond regions, and be realistic about your own situation. In other words, be willing to sell or *swap* your bonds for the following reasons:

- To minimize taxes or take a tax loss
- To consolidate odd lots
- To improve credit quality

- To increase yields from lower-rated bonds
- To extend maturity or lock in higher yield
- To shorten maturity
- To diversify geographically
- To diversify into varied types of bonds
- To achieve a capital gain

For example, you might switch to higher-coupon bonds if you think interest rates will rise, and switch to lower-coupon bonds if interest rates start to fall. Remember, however, that you will usually have to pay various costs and a service charge to swap your bonds. Always make sure the costs do not outweigh the advantage of swapping.

Finally, during periods of sharp interest-rate rises or soaring inflation, you might switch out of the bond market into non-fixed-income securities or money market funds. Or you might buy shorter securities.

If you want to sell your bonds the way the best professional investors do, then ask your bond dealer to put your bonds out with a broker. That way you will be sure your bonds are seen by all the professional buyers in the market, and you will have the best opportunity to obtain the most competitive price for your bonds.

In this book, we have discussed many aspects of investing in municipal bonds, including the advantages and the risks. Consider all of them before you plunge in. You could be well rewarded!

1

MORAL-OBLIGATION BONDS

Moral-obligation bonds have been referred to in passing in various chapters in this book. They are discussed here in more detail because they are important to those interested in investing in the housing bond market.

Moral-obligation bonds are *not* backed by a state government's full faith, credit, or taxing power. Nevertheless, moral-obligation bonds have a kind of pledge of support from the state government in case the bonds are defaulted. Technically, the state has a reserve fund which may be used to support the debt issue. Typically a debt service fund will have the money to pay the maximum interest and principal redemption needed in any year in the future. While there are now a number of different types of these bonds in the different states, the general concept of moral-obligation bonds remains the same, dating from the time they were first issued by the New York State Urban Development Corporation in 1968. In short, moral-obligation bonds are issued as a means of circumventing the tightening restrictions imposed by taxpayers and legislators on governments issuing new bonds or incurring other credit obligations without voter approval. They enabled many states to issue bonds, and to incur further debt, that would have been prohibited by the existing legislation. These bonds are controversial. Some claim they are an important means for states to expand the financing of projects; others see them as a means to avoid the constraints of restrictive laws.

Despite the restrictive laws, state governments have, in various instances, backed up moral-obligation bonds when they went into default. This happened to New York's Urban Development Corporation, and New York State stepped in to rescue it, even though it was not legally obligated to do so. New York State did so in order to protect its own ability to borrow. Over the years, states have backed up their moral-obligation bonds well in advance of the time the bonds were due to mature and even when they had no "moral obligation" to do so. Standard & Poor's, accordingly, rates these bonds only one full category below the state's general-obligation bonds.

2

U.S. GOVERNMENT HOUSING ACT

Sections 8–11(b) of the U.S. Government Housing Act provide complete financing for Section 8 projects, but they can be used only for multifamily apartment buildings. Public housing agencies rely on the sections as do cities, districts, and nonprofit corporations. Under Sections 8–11(b), bonds must be offered for permanent financing. They must cover the development cost of a project, debt service for one year, capitalized interest (which is usually the negative arbitrage of the issuing authority during the construction period), and the expenses involved in offering the bonds.

Bond issues backed by guarantees from Sections 8–11(b) have generally been sold with closed-end indentures. Since these bond issues usually involve only one housing project, which is the only source of revenue to pay off the bonds, the rating agencies and investors use a feasibility study to provide information on this very limited portfolio.

The financial analysis of these bond issues should forecast two years of operations of the project once it is built. The forecast should include all reserves and their funding, the working capital to cover debt services, specified balance sheets, income statements, and statements of the anticipated flow of funds. If available, the feasibility study should include a market survey of future levels of occupancy, "rent up," and in general, the forecast demand and rate of delinquency in rent payments.

APPENDIX
3

STATE TAXES ON OUT-OF-STATE BONDS

PERSONAL PROPERTY TAX, INCOME TAX AND TOTAL EFFECTIVE TAX

State	Personal property tax[a] (nominal rate)	Income tax (top nominal rate)	Total effective tax rate in 50% federal bracket*
Alabama	0.25%[b]	5.0%	4.0%
Arizona	none	8.0%	4.2%
Arkansas	none	7.0%	3.5%
California	none	11.0%	5.5%
Colorado	none	8.0%	4.7%
Connecticut	none	13.0%	6.5%

*Calculated for 9% coupon bond at par. The effect of some personal property taxes, as a percentage of income, varies as coupon rates change.

a–Percent of market value, unless otherwise footnoted as follows: b–Percent of par value: c–Percent of annual coupon income

States with personal property tax and/or income tax which do not apply to municipal bonds: Dist. of Col., Neb., N.M., Utah, and Vt.

States with no personal property tax or income tax: Alaska, Conn., Nev., S.D., Tex., Wash., and Wyo.

Reprinted with permission from Steven J. Hueglin and Karyn Ward, *Guide to State and Local Taxation of Municipal Bonds.* Copyright © 1981 by Gabriele, Hueglin & Cashman, Inc. Updated 1984 by the authors.

State	Personal property tax[a] (nominal rate)	Income tax (top nominal rate)	Total effective tax rate in 50% federal bracket*
Delaware	none	13.5%	6.8%
Florida	0.10%	none	0.6%
Georgia	0.10%	6.0%	3.5%
Hawaii	none	11.0%	4.9%
Idaho	none	7.5%	3.8%
Illinois	none	2.5%	1.3%
Indiana	0.20%	NA	1.1%
Iowa	none	13.0%	6.9%
Kansas	2.25%	9.0%	6.5%
Kentucky	0.25%	6.0%	4.5%
Louisiana	none	6.0%	3.1%
Maine	none	10.0%	5.0%
Maryland	none	5.0%	3.8%
Massachusetts	none	10.75%	5.4%
Michigan	3.50%[c]	6.1%	4.8%
Minnesota	none	17.6%	9.6%
Mississippi	none	5.0%	2.5%
Missouri	none	6.0%	3.3%
Montana	none	11.0%	5.8%
New Hampshire	none	5.0%	2.5%
New Jersey	none	3.5%	1.8%
New York	none	14.0%	7.0%
North Carolina	0.25%	7.0%	4.8%
North Dakota	none	9.0%	5.1%
Ohio	−2.05%	9.1%	2.6%
Oklahoma	none	6.0%	3.0%
Oregon	none	10.8%	5.4%
Pennsylvania	0.40%	2.35%	3.4%
Rhode Island	none	26.75%	5.8%
South Carolina	none	7.0%	3.5%
Tennessee	none	6.0%	3.0%
Virginia	none	5.75%	2.9%
West Virginia	0.64%	13.4%	9.8%
Wisconsin	none	11.0%	5.5%

THE ADVANTAGE OF IN-STATE BONDS (PAR BONDS)

Calculated for a 9% bond selling at 100 to yield 9.00% to maturity. Calculated to take account of income tax and personal property tax but not federal or state capital gains tax. Top state brackets and 50% federal bracket assumed.

State	Net yield after tax on in-state bond	Net yield after tax on out-of-state bond	Yield advantage of in-state bond (in basis points)
Alabama	9.00%	8.64%	36
Alaska	9.00%	9.00%	none
Arizona	9.00%	8.62%	38
Arkansas	9.00%	8.69%	31
California	9.00%	8.51%	49
Colorado	9.00%	8.58%	42
Connecticut	9.00%	8.42%	58
Delaware	9.00%	8.39%	61
Dist. of Columbia	9.00%	9.00%	none
Florida	9.00%	8.95%	05
Georgia	9.00%	8.68%	32
Hawaii	9.00%	8.56%	44
Idaho	9.00%	8.66%	34

State	Net yield after tax on in-state bond	Net yield after tax on out-of-state bond	Yield advantage of in-state bond (in basis points)
Illinois	8.88%	8.88%	none
Indiana	9.00%	8.90%	10
Iowa	8.38%	8.38%	none
Kansas	8.54%	8.42%	12
Kentucky	9.00%	8.59%	41
Louisiana	9.00%	8.72%	28
Maine	9.00%	8.55%	45
Maryland	9.00%	8.66%	34
Massachusetts	9.00%	8.51%	49
Michigan	9.00%	8.57%	43
Minnesota	9.00%	8.14%	86
Mississippi	9.00%	8.78%	22
Missouri	9.00%	8.70%	30
Montana	9.00%	8.48%	52
Nebraska	9.00%	9.00%	none
Nevada	9.00%	9.00%	none
New Hampshire	9.00%	8.78%	22
New Jersey	9.00%	8.84%	16
New Mexico	9.00%	9.00%	none
New York	9.00%	8.37%	63
North Carolina	9.00%	8.57%	43
North Dakota	9.00%	8.50%	50
Ohio	9.18%	8.77%	41
Oklahoma	8.73%	8.73%	none
Oregon	9.00%	8.51%	49
Pennsylvania	9.00%	8.69%	31
Rhode Island	9.00%	8.48%	52
South Carolina	9.00%	8.69%	31
South Dakota	9.00%	9.00%	none
Tennessee	9.00%	8.73%	27
Texas	9.00%	9.00%	none
Utah	9.00%	9.00%	none

State	Net yield after tax on in-state bond	Net yield after tax on out-of-state bond	Yield advantage of in-state bond (in basis points)
Vermont	9.00%	9.00%	none
Virginia	9.00%	8.74%	26
Washington	9.00%	9.00%	none
West Virginia	9.00%	8.40%	60
Wisconsin	8.50%	8.50%	none
Wyoming	9.00%	9.00%	none

5

THE ADVANTAGE OF IN-STATE BONDS (DISCOUNTS)

Calculated for a 5.00% coupon bond due in ten years selling at 68.84 to yield 10.00% to maturity. Yield after federal gains tax only, in the 50% federal tax bracket = 9.51%. Top state brackets and 50% federal bracket assumed.

State	Net yield after tax on in-state bond	Net yield after tax on out-of-state bond	Yield advantage of in-state bond (in basis points)
Alabama	9.46%	9.12%	34
Alaska	9.51%	9.51%	none
Arizona	9.49%	9.21%	28
Arkansas	9.42%	9.19%	23
California	9.44%	9.08%	36
Colorado	9.48%	9.18%	30
Connecticut	9.51%	9.05%	46
Delaware	9.44%	9.00%	44
Dist. of Columbia	9.46%	9.46%	none
Florida	9.51%	9.21%	30
Georgia	9.48%	9.23%	25
Hawaii	9.46%	9.14%	32

State	Net yield after tax on in-state bond	Net yield after tax on out-of-state bond	Yield advantage of in-state bond (in basis points)
Idaho	9.47%	9.23%	24
Illinois	9.39%	9.39%	none
Indiana	9.50%	9.36%	14
Iowa	9.02%	9.02%	none
Kansas	9.15%	9.06%	9
Kentucky	9.49%	9.15%	34
Louisiana	9.49%	9.29%	20
Maine	9.46%	9.13%	33
Maryland	9.51%	9.23%	28
Massachusetts	9.46%	9.09%	37
Michigan	9.48%	9.28%	20
Minnesota	9.43%	8.78%	65
Mississippi	9.45%	9.28%	17
Missouri	9.49%	9.28%	21
Montana	9.47%	9.06%	41
Nebraska	9.47%	9.47%	none
Nevada	9.51%	9.51%	none
New Hampshire	9.51%	9.35%	16
New Jersey	9.51%	9.34%	17
New Mexico	9.47%	9.47%	none
New York	9.41%	8.81%	60
North Carolina	9.42%	9.06%	36
North Dakota	9.46%	9.13%	33
Ohio	9.29%	9.59%	30
Oklahoma	9.29%	9.29%	none
Oregon	9.43%	9.08%	35
Pennsylvania	9.51%	9.18%	33
Rhode Island	9.46%	9.08%	38
South Carolina	9.47%	9.24%	23
South Dakota	9.51%	9.51%	none
Tennessee	9.51%	9.32%	19
Texas	9.51%	9.51%	none
Utah	9.49%	9.49%	none

State	Net yield after tax on in-state bond	Net yield after tax on out-of-state bond	Yield advantage of in-state bond (in basis points)
Vermont	9.46%	9.46%	none
Virginia	9.48%	9.29%	19
Washington	9.51%	9.51%	none
West Virginia	9.47%	8.72%	75
Wisconsin	9.02%	9.02%	none
Wyoming	9.51%	9.51%	none

Reprinted with permission from Steven J. Hueglin and Karyn Ward, *Guide to State and Local Taxation of Municipal Bonds*. Copyright © 1981 by Gabriele, Hueglin & Cashman, Inc. Updated 1984 by the authors.

APPENDIX
6

THE EFFECTS OF 1984 CONGRESSIONAL ACTIONS ON INDUSTRIAL DEVELOPMENT AND, MORTGAGE-BACKED BONDS, AND THE INCLUSION OF MUNICIPAL SECURITY INCOME IN THE CALCULATION OF SOCIAL SECURITY BENEFITS

Because of widespread national concern about how the United States could cope with $200 billion yearly federal deficits, and the prospect of their ever increasing, by the summer of 1984 there were rising pressures on Congress and the White House to propose drastic tax reforms. For example, there were widespread moves to try to close the numerous "tax loopholes" that over the years had been enacted into law to aid or protect special-interest groups and the wealthiest taxpayers from certain taxes. One area of tax loopholes involved the growth of tax-exempt securities known as *industrial development bonds*, which are ultimately backed not by the municipality (as are other municipal securities), but by a private corporation. Bonds of this kind had been issued for such purposes as pollution-control facilities at factories, the building of convention centers and airports, as well as the building of warehouses, factories, and even stores in less economically developed areas, or in ghettos, in order to spur employment and economic growth there.

Because of these looming deficits, congressional pressure mounted to inaugurate various types of flat tax systems and a drastic elimination of abuses of the tax-exemption provisions from the IRS Code—including abusive examples of industrial development bond projects that were purely commercial in nature, did not serve a true public purpose, and whose recent proliferation was producing an unjustified drain on the United States Treasury by syphoning off needed tax revenues with their blanket tax exemption. Critics argued that while a legitimate public purpose could be served by offering tax-exempt financing for multi-family housing, mass transit, and other such facilities via corporations or authorities, the current onrush of industrial development bond financings were just enriching private developers, millionaires, and the wealthiest investors, it was argued, paid virtually no tax at all because so much of their total wealth was invested in tax-free industrial development bonds for shopping centers.

And, in fact, there *had* been real abuses of the public-purpose doctrine that was used to justify giving tax exemption to municipal securities financing such construction projects as luxury condominiums and such commercial ventures as the building of K-mart Shopping Centers, and scores of McDonald's fast-food franchises. Certain tax-exempt municipal industrial development bonds were even used in rare incidents to construct pornographic movie theaters, "go-go parlors," and pornographic bookstores. Thus, in the summer of 1984 Congress moved to put a fairly rigid cap on these tax-free securities abuses. They agreed in a House-Senate conference to national legislation that would create a limit on the total dollar amount of these industrial development bonds that could be issued by each state. The House-Senate conferees set the ceiling or total amount of industrial development bonds allowed per state annually at a multiple of $150 per person in each state. States could then individually choose how they wished to allocate this total dollar amount of industrial development bond financing, and which projects they considered to have highest priority or greatest public need.

But, in fact, this was not a rigid ceiling on industrial development bond issuance by particular states because, simultaneously, the House-Senate conferees spelled out a number of explicit and potentially wide-ranging exceptions to the new state limits. Exempted from these caps or limits would be hefty tax-exempt securities offerings for multi-family housing, mass transit, and many other "exempt facilities," as well as many industrial development bond projects that were officially "owned" and "managed" by the municipality. Since many industrial development projects have been officially owned by municipalities and leased to private concerns or corporations, this represents a very sizeable exception to the new state caps.

Investors' fears that Congress was somehow going to cap all tax-free bonds, grew despite all the evidence that these so-called rigid state caps on industrial development bonds would not much restrain such financing. These investors' fears were fueled by certain TV newscasters who rushed to report this complicated congressional tax reform, and incorrectly reported that it was a national measure to tax municipal bonds or cap the amount of tax-free municipals that an individual could own. Many of these TV reports were quite inaccurate but, nevertheless, a totally unfounded fear persisted that Congress was going to pull the rug out from under all municipal securities by abolishing tax exemption or putting a cap or limit of $150 on the municipals a person could own. This was not the case, but such rumors have continued.

Therefore, it is necessary to state clearly that this $150 per capita limit refers only to that narrow area of the whole municipal bond market known as industrial development bonds. *It does not refer to any limit on what you as an investor can own, but only to a limit on the total dollar value of such industrial bonds that a state can issue, which is a multiple of $150 per person in the state, or up to $200 million if it is a state with a small population.* And in fact, because this new law explicitly stated that various exempt facilities would not be included in these state limits, it is clear that even new municipal bond issuance for industrial development projects will greatly exceed these so-called state caps.

This specific area of the municipal bond market that is known as industrial development bonds accounts today for only about 10 percent of all new municipal securities sold each year. And although it is true that it was among the fastest-growing sectors of the municipal market up until this year, it is unlikely that the volume of newly issued industrial development bonds will suddenly decline because of the new law. In fact, many expect their issuance to continue to grow despite the "state caps," because industrial development projects aimed at luring new industry, trade, and economic growth into cities, states, and regions are among the most talked about proposals today at all levels of government.

In the very same new bill that establishes these "state caps," the legislators reinstated the authority of state and local government organizations to issue mortgage-backed revenue bonds. The official authority to issue such bonds had expired on January 1, 1984. Had Congress been serious about any total cutback in tax-free bond issuance, they could just have allowed that authority to issue mortgage-backed bonds to die when it officially expired. Instead, Congress brought those mortgage-backed bonds back to life for at least four more years, and billions of dollars of such bonds are now waiting in the wings to be issued and sold to the public. Although this provision of the law was argued to be a trade-off for the rigid state caps in the same congressional bill, most experts saw this rebirth of the mortgage-backed bonds—which are used to subsidize mortgages for low- and middle-income families—as a way to indicate that these clearly public-purpose facilities for housing, and other real needs, would be granted tax-free bond financing approval.

A quite different congressional row continued to fester concerning the congressional legislation that reformed the Social Security law in 1983. This amended the Social Security rules concerning *the counting or including* of individual investors' interest income from tax-free municipal securities as part of their total income when calculating the amount of Social Security payments these individuals were entitled to receive. Some critics attacked this change in the Social Security law as an illegal and unconstitutional federal tax upon municipal bonds. Although this entire issue generated much heat and lobbying pressure in Washington and state capitals, it is really one that will involve relatively small dollar amounts and is unlikely to have the drastically harmful effects that its critics fear it will have on impoverished Social Security-dependent retirees. In fact, since it is primarily the wealthier investors who have substantial interest income from owning many tax-free municipal securities who will be most affected by this new law, it is unlikely that their survival is dependent upon receiving the full amount of their Social Security check each month. Most such well-off investors will be well able to withstand the few dollars less in their Social Security payments. But there are certainly a number of cases of real harm among retirees *who do need their full Social Security checks*. These people will be directly and adversely affected by counting their meager interest income from their few municipal bonds in their calculations of their total yearly income and elligibility for Social Security. Furthermore, this whole issue directly involves United States constitutional issues and certainly deserves continuing public debate. In conclusion, however, I wish to emphasize that the total dollar amount that each individual investor in tax-free bonds might suffer in lost Social Security payments per year is relatively small—in the vast number of cases it should be well under $2,000.

GLOSSARY

ACCRUED INTEREST—Interest due on a bond from the last interest payment to the present.

AD VALOREM TAX—The tax levied on real property.

AMORTIZE—Payment of a debt periodically from funds received for that purpose.

ASSESSED VALUATION—The estimated value of property established as a basis for levying a tax.

BASIS BOOK—Mathematical tables used to calculate yield percentages in relation to dollar values of municipal bonds.

BASIS POINT—The returns on municipal securities are usually given in terms of basis points. One basic point is equal to 1/100 of 1 percent.

BASIS PRICE—The value of a security quoted in yield or percentage of return on the investment.

BEARER SECURITY—A security that is assumed to be owned by the person who possesses it. These securities are freely and easily negotiable, since ownership can be quickly transferred from seller to buyer (or stolen).

BOND—A promise to pay the dollar amount printed on the face of the ceritificate on a specified date with interest.

BOND ANTICIPATION NOTES—Notes issued by states and municipalities that are to be funded eventually through the sale of a bond issue.

BOND BANK—In a few states, organizations exist to buy issues of bonds of municipalities that they finance.

BOND FUNDS—Companies invested in diversified portfolios of bonds.

BROKERS—Brokers buy and sell as agents for dealers and dealer banks.

CALLABLE BONDS—Bonds that may be redeemed at the option of the issuer before maturity date, often at a premium.

CLOSED LIEN—A bond issuer makes a commitment not to pledge funds for more than one use.

COMPETITIVE UNDERWRITING—Underwriters or syndicates of underwriters submit sealed bids to purchase securities from an agency or authority. This is contrasted with a negotiated underwriting.

CONCESSION—The profit that an underwriter permits a nonmember of the underwriting syndicate.

CONFIRMATION—Written confirmation of an oral transaction in municipal securities concerning terms of the transaction.

COUPON—The interest that the borrower will pay the bondholder. Coupon is also the certificate of interest that the municipal borrowers will pay the bondholders.

COVERAGE—The margin of security for payment of debt service, usually on revenue bonds, reflecting the number of times by which earnings exceed debt service.

CURRENT YIELD—The percentage ratio of interest to the price of the bond.

DATED DATE—The date on which the bonds are issued.

DEALER—A securities firm or bank that underwrites, trades, and sells municipal securities.

DEBT LIMIT—The statutory or constitutional maximum debt that an issuer can legally incur.

DEBT RATIO—The ratio of the issuer's debt to a measure of value, such as assessed valuations or real value.

DEBT SERVICE—The money needed to pay interest and principle on a bond issue.

DEFAULT—Failure to pay principle or interest.

DENOMINATION—The principal amount due as stated on the bond certificate.

DISCOUNT—The price of a security bought below the par value.

DOLLAR BOND—A bond that is quoted and traded in dollar prices rather than in terms of yield.

DOUBLE-BARRELED BOND—A bond secured by the pledge of two or more sources.

DOUBLE EXEMPT SECURITIES—Securities that are exempt from state as well as federal income taxes.

FACE AMOUNT—The par value (the principal or maturity value) of a security appearing on the face of the instrument.

GENERAL-OBLIGATION BOND—A bond secured by the issuer's full faith and credit, and taxing power.

GROSS DEBT—The sum of a municipal debtor's obligation.

INDUSTRIAL-REVENUE BOND—A security issued by governments or agencies to construct or purchase industrial facilities to be leased to a private corporation and backed by the corporation, *not* by the municipality.

INTEREST—Money paid for the use of money. Municipal bond interest payment is usually expressed as an annual percentage rate.

ISSUER—A state, political subdivision, agency, or authority that borrows money through the sale of bonds or notes.

LEGAL OPINION—An opinion about the legality of a securities issue under the laws that affect it.

LIMITED-TAX BOND—A bond secured by a tax that is limited as to rate or amount.

MARKETABILITY—The ease with which a security can be traded in the secondary market.

MATURITY—The date when the principal amount of a security becomes due and payable.

MORAL-OBLIGATION BOND—A municipal security backed by project revenues and not backed by the full faith and credit of a state, but by the state to replenish the reserve fund if necessary.

MORTGAGE REVENUE BOND—A tax-exempt security to finance or purchase loans for single-family residences.

MUNICIPAL BOND FUND—Tax-exempt funds providing management of a portfolio with differing dates of maturity.

MUNICIPAL BOND TRUST—Unit investment trusts consisting of bonds that are held until maturity or until they are called.

MUNICIPAL SECURITIES REPRESENTATIVES—Professionals required to pass qualifying examination under the rules of the Municipal Securities Rulemaking Board. This group includes individuals who underwrite, trade, or sell municipal securities and give advice to investors in municipal securities.

NEGOTIATED UNDERWRITING—One underwriter or a group

of underwriters who undertake to sell bonds to investors after being assigned the bonds without a competitive bid.

NET DIRECT DEBT—The debt of a municipality aside from self-supporting debt, sinking funds, tax-anticipation notes, and revenue-anticipation notes.

NET INTEREST COST—The basis by which potential underwriters decide their issues of municipal securities. They also rely on a determination of the true interest cost.

NEW ISSUE MARKET—Market for new municipal bonds and notes.

NON-CALLABLE BOND—A bond that cannot be redeemed before its specified maturity date.

NOTES—Short-term promises secured by specific taxes, federal and state aid payments, and bond proceeds.

NOTICE OF SALE—A bond issuer's description of an upcoming bond issue and a request for bids.

OFFERING PRICE—The price at which dealers offer a new issue.

OFFICIAL STATEMENT—A bond issuer's description of the security and finances for a new issue.

OVERLAPPING DEBT—The part of an obligation of government units for which residents of a particular municipality are responsible (such as services or facilities shared by several municipalities).

OVER-THE-COUNTER MARKET (OTC)—A securities market that is composed of dealers who negotiate the price of bonds instead of relying on an auction system as a stock exchange does.

PAR VALUE—The dollar value of a bond or note when it matures.

PAYING AGENT—A designated bank or other institution that will pay the principal on a bond.

POLLUTION CONTROL BOND—Bonds issued to finance the construction of air- or water-pollution control facilities or sewage- or solid waste–disposal facilities backed by the credit of a corporation or authority of the pollution control entity rather than the credit of the municipality.

PREMIUM—The value of a security above its principal amount.

PRIMARY MARKET—The market for new issues of municipal bonds.

PRINCIPAL—The price of a bond to be paid at maturity.

PROJECT NOTES—Short-term tax-exempt securities offered by and backed by the U.S. Department of Housing and Urban Development for local housing and urban renewal projects.

RATINGS—Relative indications of credit quality estimated by Moody's, Standard & Poor's, and Fitch.

REFUNDING—The redemption of a bond issue and the offer of a new bond issue at terms more favorable to the issuer.

REGISTERED BOND—A bond whose owner is registered with the issuer or its agents.

REVENUE-ANTICIPATION NOTES (RAN)—Securities backed by the anticipation of future revenue.

REVENUE BOND—Bonds payable solely from revenues to be derived from a project that the proceeds from the bond sale financed.

SCALE—Reoffering of a serial issue of bonds to the public with the price or yields for each maturity.

SECONDARY MARKET—A market in which issues previously offered are bought and sold.

SELF-SUPPORTING DEBT—Municipal or state debt incurred for a public project, like a parking lot, that entails no tax support other than the revenue received from the tolls or fees returned from the use of the project.

SERIAL ISSUE—An issue part of which matures annually or at some other time interval.

SINKING FUND—A fund set aside by an issuer to retire debt.

SPECIAL-TAX BOND—A bond backed by a specific tax pledge, such as sales tax.

SPREAD—(1) Difference between bid and asked prices, or between yields on or prices of two securities of different bonds and maturities, or (2) the range between the price gained by the issuer and that paid.

SUBDIVISION—A unit of government, such as a county, town, city, or village.

SWAP—A transaction in which an investor sells one security and buys another in the same price range.

SYNDICATE—A group of investment bankers and/or banks who underwrite an issue and offer it for public sale.

TAKE-DOWN—The discount allowed to a member of a syndicate on any bonds he or she sells from the account.

TAX-ANTICIPATION NOTES—Securities backed by the anticipation of future tax receipts.

TAX BASE—Property and resources within a government or authority that it can tax.

TAX-EXEMPT BOND—A bond whose interest is exempt from federal tax and possibly state and local taxes as well.

TAX-EXEMPT BOND FUND—Registered unit investment trusts, the assets of which are invested in a diversified portfolio of interest-bearing municipal bonds issued by states, cities, counties, and other authorities.

TERM BOND—A bond that has a single maturity date.

TOTAL BONDED DEBT—All of the debt of a municipality issued as bonds.

TOTAL DIRECT DEBT—The sum of bonded and other debt (typically short-term notes) of a municipality.

TRADING MARKET—The secondary market for bonds already issued.

TRIPLE-TAX-EXEMPT BONDS—Municipal securities that are exempt from taxation by federal, state, and local governments.

TRUE INTEREST COST—A method to calculate the value of new issues that includes an estimate of the cost of money over time.

TRUSTEE—A bank serving for the issuer as the custodian of funds and representative of bondholders to enforce the bond contract.

UNDERWRITE—To purchase a bond or note issue to resell to the general public.

UNIT INVESTMENT TRUST (MUNICIPAL)—A fixed portfolio of tax-exempt bonds sold in fractional, undivided interests (usually $1,000).

UNLIMITED TAX BONDS—Bonds that are not limited in rate or amount and are secured by the pledge of real property taxes.

YIELD TO MATURITY—The average annual return if the security is held to maturity and all interest is received over the life of the security.

I N D E X

191